MW01063564

Aquinas's Lenten Meditations

Also by St. Thomas Aquinas
from Sophia Institute Press:

The Aquinas Prayer Book

The Aquinas Catechism

Aquinas's Shorter Summa

St. Thomas Aquinas

Aquinas's Lenten Meditations

40 Days with the Angelic Doctor

Translated by Fr. Philip Hughes

SOPHIA INSTITUTE PRESS

Manchester, New Hampshire

Sophia Institute Press
Box 5284, Manchester, NH 03108
1-800-888-9344

www.SophiaInstitute.com

Sophia Institute Press® is a registered trademark of Sophia Institute.

paperback ISBN 978-1-64413-706-2

ebook ISBN 978-1-64413-707-9

Library of Congress Control Number: 2022944857

Third printing

Contents

Ash Wednesday and the Days Following

First Week of Lent

Second Week of Lent

Third Week of Lent

Fourth Week of Lent

Fifth Week of Lent

Holy Week

Aquinas's Lenten Meditations

Ash Wednesday and
the Days Following

Ash Wednesday

Death

By one man sin entered into this world, and by sin death.

—Romans 5:12

1. If, for some wrongdoing, a man is deprived of some benefit once given to him, that he should lack that benefit is the punishment of his sin.

Now, in man's first creation, he was divinely endowed with this advantage: that, as long as his mind remained subject to God, the lower powers of his soul were subjected to the reason and the body was subjected to the soul.

But because, by sin, man's mind moved away from its subjection to God, it followed that the lower parts of his mind ceased to be wholly subjected to the reason. From this there followed such a rebellion of the bodily inclination against the reason, that the body was no longer wholly subject to the soul.

Whence followed death and all the bodily defects. For life and wholeness of body are bound up with this: that the body is wholly subject to the soul, as a thing that can be made perfect is subject to that which makes it perfect. So it comes about that, conversely, there are such things as death, sickness, and every other bodily defect, for such misfortunes are bound up with an incomplete subjection of body to soul.

2. The rational soul is of its nature immortal, and therefore death is not natural to man insofar as man has a soul. It is natural to his body, for the body, since it is formed of things contrary to each other in nature, is necessarily liable to corruption, and it is in this respect that death is natural to man.

Aquinas's Lenten Meditations

But God, who fashioned man, is all powerful. And hence, by an advantage conferred on the first man, He took away that necessity of dying that was bound up with the matter of which man was made. This advantage was, however, withdrawn through the sin of our first parents.

Death is then natural, if we consider the matter of which man is made, and it is a penalty, inasmuch as it happens through the loss of the privilege whereby man was preserved from dying.

3. Sin—Original Sin and actual sin—is taken away by Christ; that is to say, by Him who is also the remover of all bodily defects. He "shall quicken also your mortal bodies, because of His Spirit that dwelleth in you" (Rom. 8:11).

But, according to the order appointed by a wisdom that is divine, it is at the time that best suits that Christ takes away both the one and the other, i.e., both sin and bodily defects.

Now, it is only right that, before we arrive at that glory of impassibility and immortality that began in Christ and was acquired for us through Christ, we should be shaped after the pattern of Christ's sufferings. It is then only right that Christ's liability to suffer should remain in us, too, for a time, as a means of our coming to the impassibility of glory in the way He Himself came to it.

Thursday

Fasting

1. We fast for three reasons:
    1. To check the desires of the flesh. So St. Paul says, "In fastings, in chastity" (2 Cor. 6:5-6), meaning that fasting is a safeguard for chastity. As St. Jerome says, "Without Ceres and Bacchus, Venus would freeze," as much as to say that lust loses its heat through spareness of food and drink.
    2. That the mind may more freely raise itself to contemplation of the heights. We read in the book of Daniel that it was after a fast of three weeks that Daniel received the revelation from God (Dan. 10).
    3. To make satisfaction for sin. This is the reason given by the prophet Joel: "Be converted to me with all your heart, in fasting, and in weeping, and in mourning" (2:12). And here is what St. Augustine writes on the matter: "Fasting purifies the soul. It lifts up the mind, and it brings the body into subjection to the spirit. It makes the heart contrite and humble, scatters the clouds of desire, puts out the flames of lust and the true light of chastity."

2. There is a commandment laid on us to fast. For fasting helps to destroy sin and to raise the mind to thoughts of the spiritual world. Each man is then bound, by the natural law of the matter, to fast just as much as is necessary to help him in these matters; which is

to say that fasting in general is a matter of natural law. To determine, however, when we shall fast and how, according to what suits and is of use to the Catholic body, is a matter of positive law. To state the positive law is the business of the bishops, and what is thus stated by them is called *ecclesiastical fasting*, in contradistinction with the natural fasting previously mentioned.

3. The times fixed for fasting by the Church are well chosen. Fasting has two objects in view:
1. The destruction of sin
2. The lifting of the mind to higher things

The times self-indicated for fasting, then, are those in which men are especially bound to free themselves from sin and to raise their minds to God in devotion. Such a time especially is that which precedes that solemnity of Easter in which Baptism is administered and sin thereby destroyed and when the burial of Our Lord is recalled, for we are buried together with Christ by baptism into death (Rom. 6:4). Then, too, at Easter most of all, men's minds should be lifted, through devotion to the glory of that eternity that Christ in His Resurrection inaugurated.

Wherefore the Church has decreed that immediately before the solemnity of Easter, we must fast and, for a similar reason, that we must fast on the eves of the principal feasts, setting apart those days as opportune to prepare ourselves for the devout celebration of the feasts themselves.

Friday

The crown of thorns

*Go forth, ye daughters of Sion, and see king Solomon in
the diadem, wherewith his mother crowned him in the day
of his espousals, and in the day of the joy of his heart.*

Canticles 3:11

This is the voice of the Church inviting the souls of the faithful to behold the marvelous beauty of her Spouse. For the daughters of Sion—who are they but the daughters of Jerusalem, holy souls; the citizens of that city that is above; those who, with the angels, enjoy the peace that knows no end and, in consequence, look upon the glory of the Lord?

1. "Go forth," shake off the disturbing commerce of this world so that, with minds set free, you may be able to contemplate him whom you love. And see King Solomon, the true peacemaker—that is to say, Christ Our Lord.

"In the diadem wherewith his mother crowned him," as though the Church said, "Look on Christ, garbed with flesh for us, the flesh He took from the flesh of His mother." For it is His flesh that is here called a diadem, the flesh that Christ assumed for us, the flesh in which He died and destroyed the reign of death, the flesh in which, rising once again, He brought to us the hope of resurrection.

This is the diadem of which St. Paul speaks: "We see Jesus ... for the suffering of death, crowned with glory and honour" (Heb. 2:9). His Mother is spoken of as crowning Him because it was Mary the Virgin who, from her own flesh, gave Him flesh.

"In the day of his espousals," that is, in the hour of His Incarnation, when He took to Himself the Church not having spot or wrinkle (Eph. 5:27), the hour when God was again joined with man. "And

Aquinas's Lenten Meditations

in the day of the joy of his heart," for the joy and the gaiety of Christ is for the human race salvation and redemption. And coming home, He calls together His friends and neighbors, saying to them, "Rejoice with me, because I have found my sheep that was lost" (Luke 15:6).

2. We can, however, refer the whole of this text simply and literally to the Passion of Christ. For Solomon, foreseeing through the centuries the Passion of Christ, was uttering a warning for the daughters of Sion—that is, for the Jewish people.

"Go forth ... and see king Solomon," that is, Christ, in His diadem, that is to say, the crown of thorns with which His mother the Synagogue has crowned Him; "in the day of His espousals," the day when He joined to Himself the Church; "and in the day of the joy of His heart," the day in which He rejoiced that by His Passion, He was delivering the world from the power of the devil. Go forth, therefore, and leave behind the darkness of unbelief, and see, understand with your minds, that He who suffers as man is really God.

Go forth, beyond the gates of your city, that you may see Him, on Mount Calvary, crucified.

Saturday

The grain of wheat

*Unless the grain of wheat falling into the
ground die, itself remaineth alone.*

—John 12:24-25

We use the grain of wheat in two ways: for bread and for seed. Here the word is to be taken in the second sense, *grain of wheat* meaning "seed" and not the matter out of which we make bread. For in this sense, it never increases so as to bear fruit. When it is said that the grain must die, this does not mean that it loses its value as seed but that it is changed into another kind of thing. So St. Paul says, "That which thou sowest is not quickened, except it die first" (1 Cor. 15:36).

1. The Word of God is a seed in the soul of man insofar as it is a thing introduced into man's soul, by words spoken and heard, in order to produce the fruit of good works: "The seed is the Word of God" (Luke 8:11). So also the Word of God garbed in flesh is a seed placed in the world, a seed from which great crops should grow, whence it is compared in St. Matthew's Gospel to a grain of mustard seed (13:31, 32).

Our Lord therefore says to us, "I came as seed, something meant to bear fruit, and therefore I say to you, 'Unless the grain of wheat falling into the ground die, itself remaineth alone'" — which is as much as to say, "Unless I die, the fruit of the conversion of the Gentiles will not follow." He compares Himself to a grain of wheat because He came to nourish and to sustain the minds of men, and to nourish and sustain are precisely what wheaten bread does for men. In the Psalms, it is written, 'That bread may strengthen man's heart' (Ps. 103:15),[1] and in St. John, "The bread that I will give is my flesh for the life of the world" (John 6:52).

2. "But if it die it bringeth forth much fruit" (John 12:25). What is here explained is the usefulness of the Passion. It is as though the Gospel said: Unless the grain fall into the earth through the humiliations of the Passion, no useful result will follow, for the grain itself remaineth alone. But if it shall die, done to death and slain by the Jews, it bringeth forth much fruit, for example:

1. *The remission of sin.* "This is the whole fruit, that the sin thereby should be taken away" (Isa. 27:9). And this is the fruit of the Passion of Christ as is declared by St. Peter: "Christ ... died once for our sins, the just for the unjust, that he might offer us to God" (1 Pet. 3:18).

2. *The conversion of the Gentiles to God.* "I have appointed you that you shall go forth and bring forth fruit and that your fruit should remain" (see John 15:16). This fruit the Passion of Christ bore: "If I be lifted up from the earth, I will draw all things to myself" (see John 12:32).

3. *The fruit of glory.* "The fruit of good labours is glorious" (Wisd. 3:15). And this fruit also the Passion of Christ brought forth: "[We have therefore] a confidence in the entering into the holies by the blood of Christ: a new and living way which He hath dedicated for us through the veil, that is to say, His flesh" (Heb. 10:19–20).

[1] RSV = Ps. 104:14–15.

First Week
of Lent

First Sunday of Lent

It was fitting that Christ should be tempted

Jesus was led by the spirit into the desert,
to be tempted by the devil.

—Matt. 4:1

Christ willed to be tempted:

1. *That He might assist us against our own temptations.* St. Gregory says, "That our Redeemer, who had come on earth to be killed, should will to be tempted was not unworthy of Him. It was indeed but just that He should overcome our temptations by His own, in the same way that He had come to overcome our death by His death."

2. To warn us that no man, however holy he be, should think himself safe and free from temptation. Whence again His choosing to be tempted after His baptism, about which St. Hilary says, "The devil's wiles are especially directed to trap us at times when we have recently been made holy, because the devil desires no victory so much as a victory over the world of grace." Whence too, Scripture warns us, "Son, when thou comest to the service of God, stand in justice and in fear, and prepare thy soul for temptation" (Ecclus. 2:1).[2]

3. To give us an example of how we should overcome the temptations of the devil, St. Augustine says, "Christ gave Himself to the devil to be tempted, that in the matter of our overcoming those same temptations, He might be of service not only by His help but by His example too."

[2] RSV = Sir. 2:1.

4. To fill and saturate our minds with confidence in His mercy. "For we have not a high priest who cannot have compassion on our infirmities, but one tempted in all things, like as we are, without sin" (Heb. 4:15).

Monday after the First Sunday of Lent

Christ had to be tempted in the desert

*He was in the desert forty days and forty
nights, and was tempted by Satan.*

—Mark 1:13

1. It was by Christ's own will that He was exposed to the temptation by the devil, as it was also by His own will that He was exposed to be slain by the limbs of the devil. Had He not so willed, the devil would never have dared to approach Him.

The devil is always more disposed to attack those who are alone, because, as is said in Sacred Scripture, "If a man shall prevail against one, two shall withstand him easily" (see Eccles. 4:12). That is why Christ went out into the desert, as one going out to a battleground, that there He might be tempted by the devil. Whereupon St. Ambrose says that Christ went into the desert for the express purpose of provoking the devil. For unless the devil had fought, Christ would never have overcome him for me.

St. Ambrose gives other reasons too. He says that Christ chose the desert as the place to be tempted for a hidden reason—namely, that he might free from his exile Adam, who, from Paradise, was driven into the desert; and again, that He did it for a reason in which there is no mystery—namely, to show us that the devil envies those who are tending toward a better life.

2. We say with St. John Chrysostom that Christ exposed Himself to the temptation because the devil most of all tempts those whom he sees alone. So in the very beginning of things, he tempted the woman when he found her away from her husband. It does not,

Aquinas's Lenten Meditations

however, follow from this that a man ought to throw himself into any occasion of temptation that presents itself.

Occasions of temptation are of two kinds. One kind arises from man's own action, when, for example, man himself goes near to sin, not avoiding the occasion of sin. That such occasions are to be avoided we know, and Holy Scripture reminds us of it: "Stay not in any part of the country round about Sodom" (see Gen. 19:17). The second kind of occasion arises from the devil's constant envy of those who are tending to better things, as St. Ambrose says, and this occasion of temptation is not one we must avoid. So, according to St. John Chrysostom, not only Christ was led into the desert by the Holy Ghost, but all the children of God who possess the Holy Ghost are led in like manner. For God's children are never content to sit down with idle hands, but the Holy Ghost ever urges them to undertake for God some great work. And this, as far as the devil is concerned, is to go into the desert, for in the desert there is none of that wickedness that is the devil's delight. Every good work is, as it were, a desert to the eye of the world and of our flesh, for good works are contrary to the desire of the world and of our flesh.

To give the devil such an opportunity of temptation as this is not dangerous, for it is much more the inspiration of the Holy Ghost, who is the promoter of every perfect work, that prompts us than the working of the devil, who hates them all.

Tuesday after the First Sunday of Lent

Christ underwent every kind of suffering

"Every kind of suffering." The things men suffer may be understood in two ways. By "kind," we may mean a particular, individual suffering; and in this sense, there was no reason why Christ should suffer every kind of suffering, for many kinds of suffering are contrary the one to the other, as, for example, to be burned and to be drowned. We are, of course, speaking of Our Lord as suffering from causes outside Himself, for to suffer the suffering effected by internal causes, such as bodily sickness, would not have become Him. But if by "kind," we mean the class, then Our Lord did suffer by every kind of suffering, as we can show in three ways:

1. *By considering the men through whom He suffered.* For He suffered something at the hands of Gentiles and of Jews, of men and even of women, as the story of the servant girl who accused St. Peter goes to show. He suffered, again, at the hands of rulers, of their ministers, and of the people, as was prophesied: "Why have the Gentiles raged, and the people devised vain things? The kings of the earth stood up, and the princes met together against the Lord and against His Christ" (Ps. 2:1–2).

   He suffered, too, from His friends, the men He knew best, for Peter denied Him and Judas betrayed Him.

2. *If we consider the things through which suffering is possible.* Christ suffered in the friends who deserted Him, and in His good name, through the blasphemies uttered against

33

Him. He suffered in the respect, in the glory, due to Him through the derision and contempt bestowed upon Him. He suffered in things, for He was stripped even of His clothing; in His soul, through sadness, through weariness, and through fear; in His body, through wounds and the scourging.

3. *If we consider what He underwent in His various parts.* His head suffered through the crown of piercing thorns, His hands and feet through the nails driven through them, His face from the blows and the defiling spittle, and His whole body through the scourging.

He suffered in every sense of His body. Touch was afflicted by the scourging and the nailing, taste by the vinegar and gall, smell by the stench of corpses as He hung on the cross in that place of the dead that is called Calvary. His hearing was torn with the voices of mockers and blasphemers, and He saw the tears of His mother and of the disciple whom He loved. If we only consider the amount of suffering required, it is true that one suffering alone, the least indeed of all, would have sufficed to redeem the human race from all its sins. But if we look at the fitness of the matter, it had to be that Christ should suffer in all the kinds of suffering.

Wednesday after the First Sunday of Lent

How great was the sorrow of Our Lord in His Passion?

Attend and see if there be any sorrow like unto my sorrow.

—Lamentations 1:12

Our Lord, as He suffered, felt really, and in His senses, that pain which is caused by some harmful bodily thing. He also felt that interior pain that is caused by the fear of something harmful and that we call sadness. In both these respects, the pain suffered by Our Lord was the greatest pain possible in this present life. There are four reasons why this was so.

1. The causes of the pain

The cause of the pain in the senses was the breaking up of the body, a pain whose bitterness derived partly from the fact that the sufferings attacked every part of His body and partly from the fact that of all species of torture, death by crucifixion is undoubtedly the most bitter. The nails are driven through the most sensitive of all places, the hands and the feet, and the weight of the body itself increases the pain every moment. Add to this the long-drawn-out agony, for the crucified do not die immediately, as do those who are beheaded.

The cause of the internal pain was:

1. All the sins of all mankind for which, by suffering, He was making satisfaction, so that, in a sense, He took them to Him as though they were His own. "The words of my sins," it says in the Psalms (21:2).

2. The special case of the Jews and the others who had had a share in the sin of His death, and especially the case of

His disciples, for whom His death had been a thing to be ashamed of.

3. The loss of His bodily life, which, by the nature of things, is something from which human nature turns away in horror.

2. We may consider the greatness of the pain according to the capacity, bodily and spiritual, for suffering of Him who suffered. In His body, He was most admirably formed, for it was formed by the miraculous operation of the Holy Ghost, and therefore its sense of touch—that sense through which we experience pain—was of the keenest. His soul, likewise, from its interior powers, had a knowledge as from experience of all the causes of sorrow.

3. The greatness of Our Lord's suffering can be considered in regard to this: that the pain and sadness were without any alleviation. For in the case of no matter what other sufferer, the sadness of mind, and even the bodily pain, is lessened through a certain kind of reasoning, by means of which there is brought about a distraction of the sorrow from the higher powers to the lower. But when Our Lord suffered, this did not happen, for He allowed each of His powers to act and suffer to the fullness of its special capacity.

4. We may consider the greatness of the suffering of Christ in the Passion in relation to this fact that the Passion and the pain it brought with it were deliberately undertaken by Christ with the object of freeing man from sin. And therefore, He undertook to suffer an amount of pain proportionately equal to the extent of the fruit that was to follow from the Passion.

From all these causes, if we consider them together, it will be evident that the pain suffered by Christ was the greatest pain ever suffered.

It was fitting that Christ should be crucified with the thieves

Christ was crucified between the thieves because such was the will of the Jews and also because this was part of God's design. But the reasons why this was appointed were not the same in each of these cases.

1. As far as the Jews were concerned, Our Lord was crucified with the thieves on either side to encourage the suspicion that He, too, was a criminal. But it fell out otherwise. The thieves themselves have left not a trace in the remembrance of man, while His Cross is everywhere held in honor. Kings, laying aside their crowns, have embroidered the cross on their royal robes. They have placed it on their crowns and on their arms. It has its place on the very altars. Everywhere, throughout the world, we behold the splendor of the Cross.

In God's plan, Christ was crucified with the thieves in order that, as for our sakes, He became accursed of the Cross, so, for our salvation, He is crucified like an evil thing among evil things.

2. Pope St. Leo the Great says that the thieves were crucified one on either side of Him so that in the very appearance of the scene of His suffering, there might be set forth that distinction that should be made in the judgment of each one of us. St. Augustine has the same thought. "The cross itself," he says, "was a tribunal. In the center was the judge. To the one side was a man who believed and was set free; to the other side, a scoffer, and he was condemned." Already

there was made clear the final fate of the living and the dead, the one class placed at His right, the other on His left.

3. According to St. Hilary, the two thieves, placed to right and to left, typify that the whole of mankind is called to the mystery of Our Lord's Passion. And since division of things according to right and left is made with reference to believers and those who will not believe, one of the two, placed on the right, is saved by justifying faith.

4. As St. Bede says, the thieves who were crucified with Our Lord represent those who, for the Faith and to confess Christ, undergo the agony of martyrdom or the severe discipline of a more perfect life. Those who do this for the sake of eternal glory are typified by the thief on the right hand. Those whose motive is the admiration of whoever beholds them imitate the spirit and the act of the thief on the left hand.

As Christ owed no debt in payment for which a man must die, but submitted to death of His own will in order to overcome death, so also He had not done anything on account of which He deserved to be put with the thieves. But of His own will, He chose to be reckoned among the wicked, that by His power, He might destroy wickedness itself. This is why St. John Chrysostom says that to convert the thief on the cross and to turn him to Paradise was as great a miracle as the earthquake.

Friday after the First Sunday of Lent

Feast of the Holy Lance
and the Nails of Our Lord

1. "One of the soldiers with a spear opened His side, and immediately there came out blood and water" (John 19:34). The Gospel deliberately says "opened" and not wounded, because through Our Lord's side there was opened to us the gate of eternal life. "After these things I looked, and behold a gate was opened in heaven" (see Apoc. 4:1).[3] This is the door opened in the ark, through which enter the animals that will not perish in the flood.

2. But this door is the cause of our salvation. Immediately there came forth blood and water — a thing truly miraculous, that, from a dead body, in which the blood congeals, blood should come forth.

This was done to show that by the Passion of Christ, we receive a full absolution, an absolution from every sin and every stain. We receive this absolution from sin through that blood that is the price of our redemption. "You were not redeemed with corruptible things as gold or silver, from your vain conversation with the tradition of your fathers: but with the precious blood of Christ as of a lamb unspotted and undefiled" (1 Pet. 1:18-19).

We were absolved from every stain by the water, which is the laver of our redemption. In the prophet Ezekiel, it is said, "I will pour upon you clean water, and you shall be cleaned from all your filthiness" (Ezek. 36:25), and in Zechariah, "There shall be a fountain

[3] RSV = Rev. 4:1.

open to the house of David, and to the inhabitants of Jerusalem for the washing of the sinner, and of the unclean woman" (Zech. 13:1).

And so these two things may be thought of in relation to two of the sacraments, the water to Baptism and the blood to the Holy Eucharist. Or both may be referred to the Holy Eucharist since, in the Mass, water is mixed with the wine—although the water is not of the substance of the sacrament.

Again, as from the side of Christ asleep in death on the Cross, there flowed that blood and water in which the Church is consecrated, so from the side of the sleeping Adam was formed the first woman, who herself foreshadowed the Church.

Saturday after the First Sunday of Lent

The love of God shown in the Passion of Christ

*God commendeth His charity towards us: because when as yet
we were sinners, according to the time, Christ died for us.*

—Romans 5:8–9

1. Christ died for the ungodly (see Rom. 5:6). This is a great thing if we consider who it is that died and on whose behalf He died. "For scarce for a just man, will one die (Rom. 5:7); that is to say, you will hardly find anyone who will die even to set free a man who is innocent; nay, it is even said, "The just perisheth, and no man layeth it to heart" (Isa. 57:1).

Rightly therefore does St. Paul say scarce will one die. There might perhaps be found one, some one rare person who, out of superabundance of courage, would be so bold as to die for a good man. But this is rare, for the simple reason that so to act is the greatest of all things. "Greater love than this no man hath," says Our Lord Himself, "that a man lay down his life for his friends" (John 15:13).

But the like of what Christ did Himself, to die for evildoers and the wicked, has never been seen. Wherefore rightly do we ask in wonderment why Christ did it.

2. If, in fact, it be asked why Christ died for the wicked, the answer is that God in this way "commendeth His charity towards us." He shows us in this way that He loves us with a love that knows no limits, for while we were as yet sinners Christ died for us.

The very death of Christ for us shows the love of God, for it was His son whom He gave to die that satisfaction might be made for us. "God so loved the world, as to give His only begotten Son" (John 3:16). And thus, as the love of God the Father for us is shown in

Aquinas's Lenten Meditations

His giving us His Holy Spirit, so also is it shown in this way, by His gift of His only Son.

The Apostle says "God commendeth," signifying thereby that the love of God is a thing that cannot be measured. This is shown by the very fact of the matter—namely, the fact that He gave His Son to die for us—and it is shown also by reason of the kind of people we are for whom He died. Christ was not stirred up to die for us by any merits of ours, "when as yet we were sinners." God (who is rich in mercy) "for His exceeding charity wherewith He loved us, even when we were dead in sins, hath quickened us together in Christ" (Eph. 2:4-5).

3. All these things are almost too much to be believed. "A work is done in your days, which no man will believe when it shall be told" (Hab. 1:5). This truth that Christ died for us is so hard a truth that scarcely can our intelligence take hold of it. Nay, it is a truth that our intelligence could in no way discover. And St. Paul, preaching, echoes Habakkuk: "I work a work in your days, a work which you will not believe, if any man shall tell it to you" (Acts 13:41).

So great is God's love for us and His grace toward us, that He does more for us than we can believe or understand.

Second Week of Lent

Second Sunday of Lent

God the Father delivered Christ to His Passion

[God] spared not even His own Son, but delivered Him up for us all.

—Romans 8:32

Christ suffered willingly, moved by obedience to His Father. Wherefore, God the Father delivered Christ to His Passion, and this in three ways:

1. Because the Father, of His eternal will, preordained the Passion of Christ as the means whereby to free the human race: so it is said in Isaiah, "The Lord hath laid on Him the iniquity of us all" (53:6), and again, "The Lord was pleased to bruise Him in infirmity" (53:10).

2. Because He inspired Our Lord with the willingness to suffer for us, pouring into His soul the love that produced the will to suffer: whence the prophet goes on to say, "He was offered because it was His own will" (53:7).

3. Because He did not protect Our Lord from the Passion but exposed Him to His persecutors: whence we read in St. Matthew's Gospel that as He hung on the Cross, Christ said, "My God, my God, why hast thou forsaken me?" (27:46), for God the Father, that is to say, had left Him at the mercy of His torturers.

To hand over an innocent man to suffering and to death against his will, compelling him to die as it were, would indeed be cruel and wicked. But it was not in this way that God the Father handed over Christ. He handed over Christ by inspiring Him with the will to suffer for us. In His so doing, the severity of God is made clear to us, that no sin is forgiven without punishment undergone; St.

Aquinas's Lenten Meditations

Paul again teaches this when he says, "God spared not His own Son" (Rom. 8:32). At the same time, God's good-heartedness is shown in the fact that whereas man could not, no matter what his punishment, sufficiently make satisfaction, God has given man Someone who can make that satisfaction for him. This is what St. Paul means by saying, "He delivered Him up for us all" (Rom. 8:32) and again when he says, "God hath proposed Christ to be a propitiation, through faith in His blood" (see Rom. 3:25). The same activity in a good man and in a bad man is differently judged inasmuch as the root from which it proceeds is different. The Father, for example, delivered over Christ, and Christ delivered Himself, and this from love; and therefore, They are praised. Judas delivered Christ from love of gain, the Jews from hatred, Pilate from the worldly fear with which he feared Caesar; and these are rightly regarded with horror. Christ, therefore, did not owe to death the debt of necessity but of charity—the charity to men by which He willed their salvation, and the charity to God by which He willed to fulfill God's will, as it says in the Gospel: "Not as I will, but as Thou wilt" (Matt. 26:39).

Monday after the Second Sunday of Lent

It was fitting that our Lord should suffer at the hands of the Gentiles

They shall deliver Him to the Gentiles to be mocked and scourged and crucified.

—Matthew 20:19

In the very manner of the Passion of Our Lord, its effects are foreshadowed. In the first place, the Passion of Our Lord had for its effect the salvation of Jews, many of whom were baptized in His death.

Secondly, by the preaching of these Jews, the effects of the Passion passed to the Gentiles also. There was thus a certain fitness in Our Lord's Passion, that, beginning with the Jews and then the Jews handing Him on, it should be completed at the hands of the Gentiles.

To show the abundance of the love that moved Him to suffer, Christ, on the very Cross, asked mercy for His tormentors. And since He wished that Jew and Gentile alike should realize this truth about His love, He wished that both should have a share in making Him suffer.

It was the Jews and not the Gentiles who offered the figurative sacrifices of the Old Law. The Passion of Christ was an offering through sacrifice, inasmuch as Christ underwent death by His own will, moved by charity. But insofar as those who put Him to death were concerned, they were not offering a sacrifice but committing a sin.

When the Jews declared, "It is not lawful for us to put any man to death" (John 18:31), they may have had many things in mind. It was not lawful for them to put anyone to death on account of the holiness of the feast they had begun to keep. Perhaps they wished Christ to be killed not as a transgressor of their own law but as an enemy of the state because He had made Himself a king, a charge concerning which they had no jurisdiction. Or again, they may have meant that they had no power to crucify, which was what they longed for, but only to stone, as they later stoned St. Stephen; or—the most likely thing of all—that their Roman conquerors had taken away their power of life and death.

Tuesday after the Second Sunday of Lent

The Passion of Christ brought about our salvation because it was a meritorious act

[They] shall deliver Him to the Gentiles to be
mocked and scourged and crucified.
—Matthew 20:19

Grace was given to Christ not only as to a particular person but also, as far as He is the head of the Church, in order that the grace might pass over from Him to His members. And the good works Christ performed, therefore, stand in this same way in relation to Him and to His members as the good works of any other man in a state of grace stand to himself.

Now, it is evident that any man who, in a state of grace, suffers for justice's sake, merits for himself, by this very fact alone, salvation. As is said in the Gospel, "Blessed are they that suffer persecution for justice's sake" (Matt. 5:10). Whence Christ, by His Passion, merited salvation not only for Himself but for all His members.

Christ, indeed, from the very instant of His conception, merited eternal salvation for us. But there still remained certain obstacles on our part, obstacles that kept us from possessing the effect of what Christ had merited. Wherefore, in order to remove these obstacles, it behooved Christ to suffer (Luke 24:46).

Now, although the love of Christ for us was not increased in the Passion, and was not greater in the Passion than before it, the Passion of Christ had a certain effect that His previous meritorious activity did not have. The Passion produced this effect not on account of any greater love shown thereby but because it was a kind of action fitted to produce that effect, as is evident from what has been said already on the fitness of the Passion of Christ.

Aquinas's Lenten Meditations

Head and members belong to one and the same person. Now, Christ is our Head, according to His divinity and to the fullness of His grace, which overflows upon others also. We are His members. What Christ, then, meritoriously acquires is not something external and foreign to us, but, by virtue of the unity of the Mystical Body, it overflows upon us too (3 Dist. 18:6).

We should know, too, that although Christ, by His death, acquired merit sufficient for the whole human race, there are special things needed for the particular salvation of each individual soul, and these each soul must itself seek out. The death of Christ is, as it were, the cause of all salvation, as the sin of the first man was the cause of all condemnation. But if each individual man is to share in the effect of a universal cause, the universal cause needs to be specially applied to each individual man.

Now, the effect of the sin of the first parents is transmitted to each individual through his bodily origin (i.e., through his being a bodily descendant of the first man). The effect of the death of Christ is transmitted to each man through a spiritual rebirth, a rebirth in which man is, as it were, conjoined with Christ and incorporated with Him.

Therefore, each individual must seek to be born again through Christ and to receive those other things in which the power of the death of Christ works.

Wednesday after the Second Sunday of Lent

The Passion of Christ brought about our salvation because it was an act of satisfaction

He is the propitiation for our sins, and not for ours
only but also for those of the whole world.

—1 John 2:2

1. Satisfaction for offenses committed is truly made when there is offered to the person offended a thing that he loves as much as, or more than, he hates the offenses committed.

Christ, however, by suffering out of love and out of obedience, offered to God something greater by far than the satisfaction called for by all the sins of all mankind, and this for three reasons. In the first place, there was the greatness of the love that moved Him to suffer. Then there was the worth of the life that He laid down in satisfaction, the life of God and man. Finally, on account of the way in which His Passion involved every part of His being and of the greatness of the suffering He undertook.

So it is that the Passion of Christ was not merely sufficient but was superabundant as a satisfaction for men's sins. It would seem indeed to be the case that satisfaction should be made by the person who committed the offense. But Head and members are, as it were, one mystical person, and therefore the satisfaction made by Christ avails all the faithful, as they are the members of Christ. One man can always make satisfaction for another, so long as the two are one in charity.

2. Although Christ, by His death, made sufficient satisfaction for Original Sin, it is not unfitting that the penal consequences of Original Sin should still remain even in those who are made sharers in Christ's redemption. This has been done fittingly and usefully, so that the penalties remain even though the guilt has been removed.

Aquinas's Lenten Meditations

- It has been done so that there might be conformity between the faithful and Christ, as there is conformity between members and Head. Just as Christ, first of all, suffered many pains and came in this way to His glory, so it is only right that His faithful should also first be subjected to sufferings and thence enter into immortality, themselves bearing, as it were, the livery of the Passion of Christ so as to enjoy a glory somewhat like to His.

- A second reason is that if men coming to Christ were straightway freed from suffering and the necessity of death, only too many would come to Him attracted rather by these temporal advantages than by spiritual things. And this would be altogether contrary to the intention of Christ, who came into this world that He might convert men from a love of temporal advantages and win them to spiritual things.

- Finally, if those who came to Christ were straightway rendered immortal and impassible, this would in a kind of way compel men to receive the Faith of Christ, and so the merit of believing would be lessened.

Thursday after the Second Sunday of Lent

The Passion of Christ brought about its effect because it was a sacrifice

A sacrifice properly so called is something done to render to God the honor specially due to Him, in order to appease Him. St. Augustine teaches this, saying, "Every work done in order that we may, in a holy union, cleave to God is a true sacrifice — every work, that is to say, related to that final good whose possession alone can make us truly happy."[4] In the Passion, Christ offered Himself for us, and it was just this circumstance, that He offered Himself willingly, that was to God the most precious thing of all, since the willingness came from the greatest possible love. Whence it is evident that the Passion of Christ was a real sacrifice.

And as He Himself adds later, the former sacrifices of the saints were so many signs, of different kinds, of this one true sacrifice. This one thing was signified through many things, as one thing is said through many words, so that it may be repeated often without beginning to weary people.

St. Augustine speaks of four things being found in every sacrifice — namely, a person to whom the offering is made, one by whom it is made, the thing offered, and those on whose behalf it is offered. These are all found in the Passion of Our Lord. It is the same person, the only, true Mediator Himself, who, through the sacrifice of peace, reconciles us to God yet remains one with Him to whom He offers,

[4] St. Augustine, *The City of God*, bk. 10, chap. 6.

who makes one with Him those for whom He offers, and is Himself the one who both offers and is offered.

It is true that in those sacrifices of the Old Law, which were types of Christ, human flesh was never offered, but it does not follow from this that the Passion of Christ was not a sacrifice. For although the reality and the thing that typifies it must coincide in one point, it is not necessary that they coincide in every point, for the reality must go beyond the thing that typifies it. It was, then, very fitting that the sacrifice in which the flesh of Christ is offered for us was typified by a sacrifice not of the flesh of man but of other animals, to foreshadow the flesh of Christ, which is the most perfect sacrifice of all. It is the most perfect sacrifice of all for these reasons:

- Since it is the flesh of human nature that is offered, it is a thing fittingly offered for men and fittingly received by men in a sacrament.
- Since the flesh of Christ was able to suffer and to die, it was suitable for immolation. Since that flesh was itself without sin, it had a power to cleanse from sin.
- Being the flesh of the very Offerer, it was acceptable to God by reason of the unspeakable love of the One who was offering His own flesh.

Whence St. Augustine says:

> What is there more suitably received by men, of offerings made on their behalf, than human flesh, and what is so suitable for immolation as mortal flesh? And what is so clean for cleansing mortal viciousness as that flesh born, without stain of carnal desire, in the womb and of the womb of a virgin? And what can be so graciously offered and received as the flesh of our sacrifice, the body so produced of our priest?[5]

[5] St. Augustine, On the Trinity, bk. 4, chap. 14.

Friday after the Second Sunday of Lent

Feast of the Holy Winding Sheet

*Joseph taking the body, wrapped it up in a clean linen
cloth and laid it in his own new monument.*

—Matthew 27:59-60

By this clean linen cloth three things are signified in a hidden way, namely:

1. The pure body of Christ: For the cloth was made of linen, which, by much pressing, is made white, and in like manner, it was after much pressure that the body of Christ came to the brightness of the Resurrection. "Thus it behooved Christ to suffer and to rise again from the dead [on] the third day" (Luke 24:46).

2. The Church, which without spot or wrinkle (Eph. 5:27), is signified by this linen woven out of many threads.

3. A clear conscience, where Christ reposes.

"And laid [Him] in his own new monument": it was Joseph's own grave, and certainly it was somehow appropriate that He who had died for the sins of others should be buried in another man's grave.

Notice that it was a new grave. Had other bodies already been laid in it, there might have been a doubt as to which had arisen. There is another fitness in this circumstance: namely, that He who was buried in this new grave was He who was born of a virgin mother. As Mary's womb knew no child before Him nor after Him, so was it with this grave. Again, we may understand that it is in a soul renewed that Christ is buried by faith, that Christ may dwell by faith in our hearts (Eph. 3:17).

St. John's Gospel adds, "Now there was in the place where He was crucified, a garden; and in the garden a new sepulchre" (John

19:41). This recalls to us that as Christ was taken in a garden and suffered His agony in a garden, so in a garden was He buried; and thereby we are reminded that it was from the sin committed by Adam in the garden of delightfulness that, by the power of His Passion, Christ set us free, and also that, through the Passion, the Church was consecrated—the Church, which, again, is as a garden closed.

Saturday after the Second Sunday of Lent

The Passion of Christ wrought our salvation by redeeming us

St. Peter says, "You were not redeemed with corruptible things as gold or silver, from your vain conversation of the tradition of your fathers: but with the precious blood of Christ, as of a lamb unspotted and undefiled" (1 Pet. 1:18-19).

St. Paul says, "Christ hath redeemed us from the curse of the law, being made a curse for us" (Gal. 3:13). He is said to be accursed in our place inasmuch as it was for us that He suffered on the Cross. Therefore, by His Passion He redeemed us.

Sin, in fact, had bound man with a double obligation.

1. An obligation that made him sin's slave: for Jesus said, "Whosoever committeth sin is the servant of sin" (John 8:34). A man is enslaved to whoever overcomes him. Therefore, since the devil, in inducing man to sin, had overcome man, man was bound in servitude to the devil.

2. A further obligation existed between man and the penalty due to the sin committed, and man was bound in this way in accord with the justice of God. This, too, was a kind of servitude, for to servitude or slavery it belongs that a man must suffer otherwise than he chooses, since the free man is the man who uses himself as he wills.

Since, then, the Passion of Christ made sufficient, and more than sufficient, satisfaction for the sins of all mankind and for the penalty due to them, the Passion was a kind of price through which we were free from both these obligations. For the satisfaction itself that by

Aquinas's Lenten Meditations

means of which one makes satisfaction, whether for oneself or for another is spoken of as a kind of price by which one redeems or buys back oneself or another from sin and from merited penalties. So in Holy Scripture it is said, "Redeem thou thy sins with alms" (Dan. 4:24).

Christ made satisfaction not indeed by a gift of money or anything of that sort but by a gift that was the greatest of all, by giving for us Himself. And thus it is that the Passion of Christ is called our redemption.

By sinning, man bound himself not to God but to the devil. As far as concerns the guilt of what he did, he had offended God and had made himself subject to the devil, assenting to his will.

Hence, he did not, by reason of the sin committed, bind himself to God; but rather, deserting God's service, he had fallen under the yoke of the devil. And God, with justice, if we remember the offense committed against Him, had not prevented this.

But, if we consider the matter of the punishment earned, it was chiefly and in the first place to God that man was bound, as to the Supreme Judge. Man was, in respect of punishment, bound to the devil only in a lesser sense, as to the torturer, as it says in the Gospel: "Lest the adversary deliver thee to the judge and the judge deliver thee to the officer" (Matt. 5:25), that is, to the cruel minister of punishments.

Therefore, although the devil unjustly, as far as was in his power, held man, whom by his lies he had deceived bound in slavery—held him bound both on account of the guilt and of the punishment due for it—it was nevertheless just that man should suffer in this way. The slavery that he suffered on account of the thing done God did not prevent, and the slavery he suffered as punishment God decreed.

Therefore, it was in regard to God's claims that justice called for man to be redeemed and not in regard to the devil's hold on us. And it was to God that the price was paid and not to the devil.

Third Week of Lent

Third Sunday of Lent

It is the Passion of Christ
that has freed us from sin

[He] hath loved us and washed us from our sins in His own blood.

—Apocalypse 1:5 (RSV = Rev. 1:5)

The Passion of Christ is the proper cause of the remission of our sins, in three ways:

1. It provokes us to love God. St. Paul says, "God commendeth His charity towards us; because when as yet we were sinners … Christ died for us" (Rom. 5:8–9). Through charity we obtain forgiveness for sin, as it says in the Gospel: "Many sins are forgiven her because she hath loved much" (Luke 7:47).

2. The Passion of Christ is the cause of the forgiveness of sins because it is an act of redemption. Since Christ is Himself our Head, He has, by His own Passion — undertaken from love and obedience — delivered us, His members, from our sins, as it were, at the price of His Passion; just as a man might, by some act of goodness done with his hands, buy himself off for a wrong thing he had done with his feet. For as man's natural body is a unity, made up of different limbs, so the whole Church, which is the Mystical Body of Christ, is reckoned as a single person with its own Head, and this Head is Christ.

3. The Passion of Christ was a thing equal to its task. For the human nature through which Christ suffered His Passion is the instrument of His divine nature. Whence all the actions and all the sufferings of that human nature wrought to drive out sin are wrought by a power that is divine.

Aquinas's Lenten Meditations

Christ, in His Passion, delivered us from our sins in a causal way; that is to say, He set up for us a thing that would be a cause of our emancipation, a thing whereby any sin might at any time be remitted, whether committed now, or in times gone by, or in time to come—much as a physician might make a medicine from which all who are sick may be healed, even those sick in the years yet to come.

But since what gives the Passion of Christ its excellence is the fact that it is the universal cause of the forgiveness of sins, it is necessary that we each make use of it for the forgiveness of our own particular sins. This is done through Baptism, Penance, and the other sacraments, whose power derives from the Passion of Christ.

By faith also we make use of the Passion of Christ, in order to receive its fruits, as St. Paul says: "Christ Jesus, whom God hath proposed to be a propitiation, through faith in His blood" (Rom. 3:24-25). But the faith by which we are cleansed from sin is not that faith that can exist side by side with sin—the faith called *formless*—but faith *formed*—that is to say, faith made alive by charity. So the Passion of Christ is not through faith applied merely to our understanding but also to our will. Again, it is from the power of the Passion of Christ that the sins are forgiven that are forgiven by faith in this way.

Monday after the Third Sunday of Lent

The Passion of Christ has delivered us from the devil

Our Lord said, as His Passion drew near, "Now shall the prince of this world be cast out. And I, if I be lifted up from the earth, will draw all things to myself" (John 12:31–32). He was lifted up from the earth by His Passion on the Cross. Therefore, by that Passion, the devil was driven out from his dominion over men.

With reference to that power that, before the Passion of Christ, the devil used to exercise over mankind, three things are to be borne in mind.

1. Man had by his sin earned for himself enslavement to the devil, for it was by the devil's temptation that he had been overcome.

2. God, whom man, in sinning, had offended, had, by His justice, abandoned man to the enslavement of the devil.

3. The devil, by his own most wicked will, stood in the way of man's achieving his salvation.

With regard to the first point, the Passion of Christ set man free from the devil's power because the Passion of Christ brought about the forgiveness of sin. As to the second point, the Passion delivered man from the devil because it brought about a reconciliation between God and man. As to the third point, the Passion of Christ freed us from the devil's power because, in his action during the Passion, the devil overreached himself. He went beyond the limits of the power over men allowed to him by God, when he plotted the death of Christ, upon whom, since He was without sin, there lay no debt payable by death. Whence St. Augustine's words:

> The devil was overcome by the justice of Christ. In Him the devil found nothing that deserved death, but nonetheless, he slew Him. And it was but just that those debtors that the devil detained should go free since they believed in Him whom, though He was under no bond to him, the devil had slain.[6]

The devil continues to exercise a power over men. He can, God permitting it, tempt them in soul and in body. There is, however, made available for man a remedy in the Passion of Christ, by means of which he can defend himself against these attacks, so that they do not lead him into the destruction of eternal death. Likewise, all those who, before the Passion of Christ, resisted the devil had derived their power to resist from the Passion, although the Passion had not yet been accomplished. But in one point, none of those who lived before the Passion had been able to escape the hand of the devil—namely, they all had to go down into Hell, a thing from which, since the Passion, all men can, by His power, defend themselves.

God also allows the devil to deceive men in certain persons, times, and places, according to the hidden character of His designs. Such, for example, will be antichrist. But there always remains, and for the age of antichrist too, a remedy prepared for man through the Passion of Christ, a power of protecting himself against the wickedness of the devils. The fact that there are some who neglect to make use of this remedy does not lessen the efficacy of the Passion of Christ.

[6] St. Augustine, *On the Trinity*, bk. 13, chap. 14.

Tuesday after the Third Sunday of Lent

Christ is truly our Redeemer

*You were redeemed with the precious blood of
Christ, as of a lamb unspotted and undefiled.*

—See 1 Peter 1:19

By the sin of our first parents, the whole human race was alienated from God, as is taught in the second chapter of the Epistle to the Ephesians. It was not from God's power that we were thereby cut off but from that sight of God's face to which His children and His servants are admitted.

Then again, we descended beneath the usurped power of the devil. Man had consented to the devil's will and thereby had made himself subject to the devil; subject, that is to say, as far as lay in man's power, for since he was not his own property but the property of another, he could not really give himself away to the devil.

By His Passion, then, Christ did two things:

1. He freed us from the power of the enemy, conquering him by virtues that were the very contraries to the vices by which he had conquered man—by humility, namely, by obedience, and by an austerity of suffering that was in direct opposition to the enjoyment of forbidden food.

2. Furthermore, by making satisfaction for the sin committed, Christ joined man with God and made him the child and servant of God.

This emancipation had about it two things that make it a kind of buying. Christ is said to have bought us back or to have redeemed us inasmuch as He snatched us from the power of the devil, as a king is said, by hard-fought battles, to redeem his kingdom that the enemy has occupied. Christ is again said to have redeemed us inasmuch as

Aquinas's Lenten Meditations

He placated God for us, paying, as it were, the price of His satisfaction on our behalf, that we might be freed both from the penalty and from the sin. This price, His precious blood, He paid that He might make satisfaction for us not to the devil but to God. Again, by the victory that His Passion was, He took us away from the devil.

The devil had indeed had dominion over us, but unjustly, since what power he had was usurped. Nevertheless, it was but just that we should fall under his yoke, seeing that it was by him that we were overcome. This is why it was necessary that the devil should be overcome by the very contrary of the forces by which he himself had overcome. For he had overcome not by violence but by a lying persuasion to sin.

The price of our redemption

You are bought with a great price.

—1 Corinthians 6:20

The indignities and sufferings anyone suffers are measured according to the dignity of the person concerned. If a king is struck in the face, he suffers a greater indignity than does a private person. But the dignity of Christ is infinite, for He is a divine person. Therefore, any suffering undergone by Him, even the least conceivable suffering, is infinite. Any suffering at all, then, undergone by Him, without His death, would have sufficed to redeem the human race.

St. Bernard says that the least drop of the blood of Christ would have sufficed for the redemption of us all. And Christ could have shed that one drop without dying. Therefore, even without dying, He could, by some kind of suffering, have redeemed—that is, bought back—all mankind.

Now in buying, two things are required: an amount equal to the price demanded and the assigning of that amount to the purpose of buying. For if a man gives a price that is not equal in value to the thing to be bought, we do not say that he has bought it but only that he has partly bought it and partly been given it. For example, if a man buys for ten shillings a book that is worth twenty shillings, he has partly bought the book, and it has partly been given to him. Or again, if he puts together a greater price but does not assign it to the buying, he is not said to buy the book. If, therefore, when we speak of the redemption and buying back of the human race, we have in view the amount of the price, we must say that any suffering undergone by Christ, even without His death, would have sufficed, because of the infinite worth of His person. If, however, we speak of the redemption with reference to the setting of the price to the purpose in hand, we have then to say that no other suffering of Christ less than His death was set by God and by Christ as the price to be paid for the redemption of mankind. And this was so for three reasons:

1. That the price of our redemption should be not only infinite in value but of the same kind as what it bought—i.e., that it should be with a death that He bought us back from death.

2. That the death of Christ would be not only the price of our redemption but also an example of courage, so that men would not be afraid to die for the truth. St. Paul makes mention of this and the preceding cause when he says, "That, through death, He might destroy him who had the empire of death [this is the first cause] ... and might deliver them, who through the fear of death were all their lifetime subject to servitude [this is the second cause]" (Heb. 2:14-15).

3. That the death of Christ might be a sacrament to work our salvation; we, that is, dying to sin, to bodily desires, and to our own will through the power of the death of Christ. These reasons are given by St. Peter when he says, "Christ also died once for our sins, the just for the unjust; that He might offer us to God, being put to death indeed in the flesh, but enlivened in the spirit" (1 Pet. 3:18).

And so it is that mankind has not been redeemed by any other suffering of Christ without His death.

But, as a matter of fact, Christ would have paid sufficiently for the redemption of mankind not only by giving His own life but by suffering any suffering, no matter how slight, if this slight suffering had been the thing divinely appointed, and Christ would thereby have paid sufficiently because of the infinite worth of His person.

Thursday after the Third Sunday of Lent

The preaching of the Samaritan woman

*The woman therefore left her waterpot
and went her way into the city.*

—John 4:28

The Samaritan woman, once Christ had instructed her, became an apostle. There are three things we can gather from what she said and what she did.

1. *The entirety of her surrender to Our Lord*
This is shown:

- From the fact that she left lying there, almost as if forgotten, that for which she had come to the well: the water and the waterpot. So great was her absorption. Hence it is said, "The woman left her water pot and went away into the city"; she went away to announce the wonderful works of Christ. She cared no longer for the bodily comforts in view of the usefulness of better things, following in this the example of the Apostles, of whom it is said that, "leaving their nets, they followed [the Lord]" (Mark 1:18). The waterpot stands for fashionable desire, by means of which men draw up pleasures from those depths of darkness signified by the well, that is, from practices that are of the earth—earthly. Those who abandon such desires for the sake of God are like the woman who left her waterpot.
- From the multitude of people to whom she tells the news—not to one nor to two or three but to a whole city. This is why she went away into the city.

Aquinas's Lenten Meditations

2. A method of preaching

She saith to the men there: Come, and see a man who has told me all things whatsoever I have done. Is not He the Christ? (John 4:29).

- She invites them to look upon Christ: "Come, and see a man": she did not straightway say that they should give themselves to Christ, for that might have been for them an occasion for blasphemy, but to begin with, she told them things about Christ that were believable and open to observation. She told them He was a man. Nor did she say, "Believe" but "Come and see," for she knew that if they, too, tasted of that well—looking, that is, upon Our Lord—they, too, would feel all she had felt. And she follows the example of a true preacher in that she attracts the men not to herself but to Christ.

- She gives them a hint that Christ is God when she says, "A man who has told me all things whatsoever I have done"—that is to say, how many husbands she had had. She is not ashamed to bring up things that make for her own confusion because the soul, once it is lighted up with the divine fire, in no way looks to earthly values and standards and cares neither for its own glory nor its shame but only for that flame that holds and consumes it.

- She suggests that this proves the majesty of Christ, saying, "Is not He the Christ?" She does not dare to assert that He is the Christ, lest she have the appearance of wishing to teach others, and the others, irritated thereat, refuse to go out to Him. Nor, on the other hand, does she leave the matter in silence, but she puts it before them questioningly, as though she left it to their own judgment. For this is the easiest of all ways of persuasion.

3. *The fruit of preaching*

"They therefore went out of the city and came unto [Christ]" (John 4:30). Hereby it is made clear to us that if we would come to Christ, we must also go out of the city, which is to say, we must lay aside all love of bodily delights.

"Let us go forth therefore to Him without the camp" (Heb. 13:13).

Friday after the Third Sunday of Lent

It is by the Passion of Christ that we have been freed from the punishment due to sin

Surely he hath borne our infirmities and carried our sorrows.

—Isaiah 53:4

By the Passion of Christ we are freed from the liability to be punished for sin with the punishment that sin calls for, in two ways: directly and indirectly.

We are freed directly inasmuch as the Passion of Christ made sufficient, and more than sufficient, satisfaction for the sins of the whole human race. Now, once sufficient satisfaction has been made, the liability to the punishment mentioned is destroyed.

We are freed indirectly inasmuch as the Passion of Christ causes the sin to be remitted, and it is from the sin that the liability to the punishment mentioned derives.

Souls in Hell, however, are not freed by the Passion of Christ, because the Passion of Christ shares its effect with those to whom it is applied by faith and by charity and by the sacraments of faith. Therefore, the souls in Hell, who are not linked up with the Passion of Christ in the way just mentioned, cannot receive its effects.

Now, although we are freed from liability to the precise penalty that sin deserves, there is, nevertheless, enjoined on the repentant sinner a penalty or penance of satisfaction; for in order that the effect of the Passion of Christ be fully worked out in us, it is necessary for us to be made of like form with Christ. Now, we are made of like form with Christ in Baptism by the sacrament, as is said by St. Paul: "We are buried together with Him by baptism into death (Rom. 6:4). Whence it is that no penalty of satisfaction is imposed on those who are baptized. Through the satisfaction made by Christ, they are wholly set free. But since Christ died once for our sins (1 Pet. 3:18), once only, man cannot a second time be made of like form with the death of Christ through the sacrament of Baptism. Therefore, those who sin again after Baptism must be made like to Christ in His suffering, through some kind of penalty or suffering that they endure in their own persons.

If death, which is a penalty due to sin, continues to subsist, the reason is this: the satisfaction made by Christ produces its effect in us insofar as we are made of one body with Him, in the way limbs are one body with the head. Now, it is necessary that the limbs be made to conform to the head. Wherefore since Christ at first had, together with the grace in His soul, a liability to suffer in His body and came to His glorious immortality through the Passion, so also should it be with us, who are His limbs. By the Passion, we are indeed delivered from any punishment as a thing fixed on us, but we are delivered in such a way that it is in the soul that we first receive the spirit of the adoption of sons, by which we are put on the list for the inheritance of eternal glory, while we still retain a body that can suffer and die. It is only afterward, when we have been fashioned to the likeness of Christ in His sufferings and death, that we are brought into the glory of immortality. St. Paul teaches this when he says, "If sons, heirs also; heirs indeed of God, and joint heirs with Christ: yet so, if we suffer with Him, that we may be also glorified with Him" (Rom. 8:17).

Saturday after the Third Sunday of Lent

The Passion of Christ reconciles us to God

We were reconciled to God by the death of His Son.

—Romans 5:10

1. The Passion of Christ brought about our reconciliation to God in two ways. It removed the sin that had made the human race God's enemy, as it says in Holy Scripture: "To God the wicked and his wickedness are alike hateful" (Wisd. 14:9) and again, "Thou hatest all the workers of iniquity" (Ps. 5:7).[7]

Secondly, the Passion was a sacrifice most acceptable to God. It is, in fact, the peculiar effect of sacrifice to be itself a thing by which God is placated, just as a man remits offenses done against him for the sake of some acknowledgment, pleasing to him, that is made. Whence it is said, "If the Lord stir thee up against me, let him accept of sacrifice" (1 Kings 26:19).[8] Likewise, the voluntary suffering of Christ was so good a thing in itself, that for the sake of this good thing found in human nature, God was pleased beyond the totality of offenses committed by all mankind, as far as concerns all those who are linked to Christ in His suffering by faith and by charity.

When we say that the Passion of Christ reconciled us to God, we do not mean that God began to love us all over again, for it is written, "I have loved thee with an everlasting love" (Jer. 31:3). We mean that, by the Passion, the cause of the hatred was taken away—on the one hand, by the removal of the sin, and on the other hand, by the compensation of a good that was more than acceptable.

[7] RSV = Ps. 5:6.
[8] RSV = 1 Sam. 26:19.

Aquinas's Lenten Meditations

2. As far as those who slew Our Lord were concerned, the Passion was indeed a cause of wrath. But the love of Christ suffering was greater than the wickedness of those who caused Him to suffer. And therefore, the Passion of Christ was more powerful in reconciling to God the whole human race than in moving God to anger.

God's love for us is shown by what it does for us. God is said to love some men because He gives them a share in His own goodness, in that Vision of His very essence, from which there follows this: that we live with Him, in His company, as His friends, for it is in that delightful condition of things that happiness (beatitude) consists.

God is then said to love those whom He admits to that Vision, either by giving them the Vision directly or by giving them what will bring them to the Vision, as when He gives the Holy Spirit as a pledge of the Vision.

It was from this sharing in the divine goodness, from this Vision of God's very essence, that man, by sin, had been removed, and it is in this sense that we speak of man as deprived of God's love.

And inasmuch as Christ, making satisfaction for us by His Passion, brought it about that men were admitted to the Vision of God, therefore it is that Christ is said to have reconciled us to God.

Fourth Week of Lent

Fourth Sunday of Lent

Christ, by His Passion, opened to us the gates of Heaven

We have a confidence in the entering into the holies by the blood of Christ.

—Hebrews 10:19

The closing of a gate is an obstacle hindering men's entrance. Now, men are hindered from entrance to the heavenly Kingdom by sin, for Isaiah says, "It shall be called the holy way: the unclean shall not pass over it" (35:8).

Now, the sin that hinders man's entrance into Heaven is of two kinds. There is, first of all, the sin of our first parents. By this sin, access to the Kingdom of Heaven was barred to man. We read in Genesis (3:24) that after the sin of our first parents God placed before the paradise of pleasure Cherubim and a flaming sword, turning every way, to keep the way of the tree of life. The other kind of hindrance arises from the sins special to each individual, the sins each man commits by his own particular action.

By the Passion of Christ, we are not only freed from the sin common to all human nature—and both the sin and its appointed penalty, since Christ pays the price on our behalf—but we are also delivered from our personal sins if we are numbered among those who are linked to the Passion by faith, by charity, and by the sacraments of the Faith. Thus it is that through the Passion of Christ, the gates of Heaven are thrown open to us. And hence, St. Paul says that "Christ, being come [a] high priest of the good things to come … by His own blood entered once into the holies, having obtained eternal redemption" (Heb. 9:11–12).

And this was foreshadowed in the Old Testament, where we read that the man-slayer shall abide there, that is, in the city of refuge, "until the death of the high priest, that is anointed with holy oil" (Num. 35:25, 28). And after he is dead, then shall the man-slayer return to his own country.

The holy fathers who, before the coming of Christ, wrought works of justice, earned their entrance into Heaven through faith in the Passion of Christ, as is written, "[The saints] by faith conquered kingdoms, wrought justice" (Heb. 11:33). By faith, too, it was that individuals were cleansed from the sins they had individually committed. But faith or goodness, no matter who the person was who possessed it, was not enough to be able to move the hindrance created by the guilty state of the whole human creation. This hindrance was removed only at the price of the blood of Christ. And therefore, before the Passion of Christ, no one could enter the heavenly Kingdom to obtain that eternal happiness that consists in the full enjoyment of God.

Christ, by His Passion, merited for us an entrance into Heaven and removed what stood in our way. By His Ascension, however, He, as it were, put mankind in possession of Heaven. And therefore it is that He ascended, opening the way before them.

Monday after the Fourth Sunday of Lent

Christ, by His Passion, merited to be exalted

He became obedient unto death, even to the death of the cross: for which cause God hath exalted Him.

—See Philippians 2:8

Merit is a thing that implies a certain equality of justice. Thus, St. Paul says, "To him that worketh, the reward is reckoned according to debt" (see Rom. 4:4).

Now, since a man who commits an injustice takes for himself more than is due to himself, it is just that he suffer loss even in what is actually due to him. If a man steals one sheep, he shall give back four, as it says in Holy Scripture (Exod. 22:1). And this is said to be merited inasmuch as, in this way, the man's evil will is punished. In the same way, the man who acts with such justice that he take less than what is due to him merits that more shall be generously superadded to what he has, as a kind of reward for his just will. So, for instance, the Gospel tells us, "He that humbleth himself shall be exalted" (Luke 14:11).

Now, in His Passion, Christ humbled Himself below His dignity in four respects:

1. In respect of His Passion and His death, things that He did not owe to undergo
2. In respect to places, for His body was placed in a grave and His soul in Hell
3. In respect to the confusion and shame that He endured
4. In respect to His being delivered over to human authority, as He said Himself to Pilate, "Thou shouldst not have any power against me, unless it were given thee from above" (John 19:11).

Aquinas's Lenten Meditations

Therefore, on account of His Passion, He merited a fourfold exaltation:

1. A glorious Resurrection: it is said in the psalm, "Thou hast known my sitting down," that is, the humiliation of my Passion, "and my rising up" (138:2).[9]

2. An ascension into Heaven: whence it is said, "He descended first into the lower parts of the earth: He that descended is the same also that ascended above all the heavens" (see Eph. 4:9-10).

3. To be seated at the right hand of the Father, with His divinity made manifest: Isaiah says, "He shall be exalted, and extolled, and shall be exceeding high. As many have been astonished at thee, so shall his visage be inglorious among men" (52:13-14), and St. Paul says, "[He became] obedient unto death, even to the death of the cross. For which cause God also hath exalted Him and hath given Him a name which is above all names" (Phil. 2:8-9), that is to say, "He shall be named God by all, and all shall pay Him reverence as God." And this is why St. Paul adds, "That in the name of Jesus every knee should bow, of those that are in heaven, on earth, and under the earth" (Phil. 2:10).

4. A power of judgment: for it is said, "Thy cause hath been judged as that of the wicked. Cause and judgment thou shalt recover" (Job 36:17).

---

[9] RSV = Ps. 139:2.

The example of Christ Crucified

Christ assumed human nature in order to restore fallen humanity. He had therefore to suffer and to do, according to human nature, the things that could serve as a remedy against the sin of the Fall.

Man's sin consists in this: that he so cleaves to bodily goods that he neglects what is good spiritually. It was therefore necessary for the Son of God to show this in the humanity He had taken, through all He did and suffered, so that men should repute temporal things, whether good or evil, as nothing; for otherwise, hindered by an exaggerated affection for them, they would be less devoted to spiritual things.

Christ, therefore, chose poor people for His parents — people nevertheless perfect in virtue — so that none of us should glory in the mere rank or wealth of our parents.

He led the life of a poor man, to teach us to set no store by wealth.

He lived the life of an ordinary man, without any rank, to wean men from an undue desire for honors.

Toil, thirst, hunger, the aches of the body: all these He endured, to encourage men, whom pleasures and delights attract, not to be deterred from virtue by the austerity a good life entails.

He went so far as to endure even death, lest the fear of death might at any time tempt man to abandon the truth. And lest any of us might dread to die even a shameful death for the truth, He chose to die by the most accursed death of all, by crucifixion.

Aquinas's Lenten Meditations

That the Son of God, made man, should suffer death was also fitting for this reason: that by His example, He stimulates our courage and so makes true what St. Peter said: "Christ suffered for us, leaving you an example that you should follow His steps" (1 Pet. 2:21).

Christ truly suffered for us, leaving us an example in anxieties, contempts, scourgings, the Cross, death itself, that we might follow in His steps. If we endure for Christ our own anxieties and sufferings, we shall also reign together with Christ in the happiness that is everlasting. St. Bernard says:

> How few are they, O Lord, who yearn to go after Thee, and yet there is no one that desireth not to come to Thee, for all men know that in Thy right hand are delights that will never fail. All desire to enjoy Thee, but not all to imitate Thee. They would willingly reign with Thee, but spare themselves from suffering with Thee. They have no desire to look for Thee, whom yet they desire to find.[10]

[10] St. Bonaventure, *De humanitate Christi*, chap. 47.

Wednesday after the Fourth Sunday of Lent

The Divine Friend

His sisters sent to Him saying, "Lord,
behold, he whom Thou lovest is sick."

—John 11:3

Three things here call for thought:

1. God's friends are from time to time afflicted in the body. It is not, therefore, in any way a proof that a man is not a friend of God that he is sick and ailing from time to time. Eliphaz argued falsely against Job when he said, "Remember, I pray thee, who ever perished being innocent? or when were the just destroyed?" (Job 4:7). The Gospel corrects this when it says, "Lord, behold, he whom thou lovest is sick," and the book of Proverbs, too, where we read, "For whom the Lord loveth, He chastiseth: and as a father in the son He pleaseth Himself" (Prov. 3:12).

2. The sisters do not say, "Lord, come and heal him." They merely explain that Lazarus is ill; they say, "He is sick." This is to remind us that, when we are dealing with a friend, it is enough to make known our necessity; we do not need to add a request. For a friend, since he wills the welfare of his friend as he wills his own, is as anxious to ward off evil from his friend as he is to ward it off from himself. This is true most of all in the case of Him who, of all friends, loves most truly. "The Lord keepeth all them that love Him" (Ps. 144:20).[11]

---

[11] RSV = Ps. 145:20.

Aquinas's Lenten Meditations

3. These two sisters, who so greatly desire the cure of their sick brother, do not come to Christ personally, as did the centurion and the man sick of the palsy. From the special love and familiarity that Christ had shown them, they had a special confidence in Him. And, possibly, their grief kept them at home, as St. Chrysostom thinks. "A friend if he continue steadfast, shall be to thee as thyself, and shall act with confidence among them of thy household" (Ecclus. 6:11).[12]

[12] RSV = Sir. 6:11.

Thursday after the Fourth Sunday of Lent

The Death of Lazarus

Lazarus our friend sleepeth.

—John 11:11

"Our friend" — for the many benefits and services he rendered us, and therefore we owe it not to fail in his necessity — "sleepeth"; therefore, we must come to his assistance: "A brother is proved in distress" (Prov. 17:17).

He sleepeth, I say, as St. Augustine says, to the Lord. But to men he was dead, and they had no power to raise him.

Sleep is a word we use with various meanings. We use it to mean natural sleep, negligence, blameworthy inattention, the peace of contemplation, and the peace of future glory, and we use it also to mean death. "We will not have you ignorant ... concerning the last sleep, that you be not sorrowful, even as others that have no hope," says St. Paul (see 1 Thess. 4:12).

Death is called "sleep" because of the hope of resurrection, and so it has been customary to give death this name since the time when Christ died and was raised again: "I have slept and have taken my rest" (Ps. 3:6).

"I go that I may awake him out of sleep" (John 11:11). In these words, Jesus gives us to understand that He could raise Lazarus from the tomb as easily as we raise a sleeper from his bed. Nor is this to be wondered at, for He is none other than the Lord who raiseth up the dead and giveth life (John 5:21). And hence He is able to say, "The hour cometh wherein all that are in the graves shall hear the voice of the Son of God" (John 5:28).

Aquinas's Lenten Meditations

"Let us go to him" (John 11:15). Here it is the mercifulness of God that we are shown. Men, living in sin and, as it were, dead—unable by any power of their own to come to Him—He mercifully draws, anticipating their desire and need. Jeremiah speaks of this when he says, "Thus saith the Lord: I have loved thee with an everlasting love, therefore have I drawn thee, taking pity on thee" (Jer. 31:3).

"Jesus therefore came and found that he had been four days already in the grave" (John 11:17). St. Augustine sees in the four-days dead Lazarus a figure of the fourfold spiritual death of the sinner. He dies, in fact, through Original Sin; through actual sin against the natural law; through actual sin against the written law; through actual sin against the law of the gospel and of grace.

Another interpretation is that the first day represents the sin of the heart: "Take away the evil of your thoughts," says Isaiah (see 1:16). The second day represents sins of the tongue: "Let no evil speech proceed from your mouth," says St. Paul (Eph. 4:29). The third day represents the sins of evil action: "Cease to do perversely" (Isa. 1:16). The fourth day stands for the sins of wicked habit.

Whatever explanation we give, Our Lord, at times, does heal those who are four days dead—that is, those who have broken the law of the gospel and are bound fast by habits of sin.

Friday after the Fourth Sunday of Lent

The Precious Blood

Through the blood of Christ the New Testament was confirmed. "This chalice is the new testament in my blood" (1 Cor. 11:25). *Testament* has a double meaning.

1. *Testament* may mean any kind of agreement or pact.

Now, God has twice made an agreement with mankind. In one pact, God promised man temporal prosperity and deliverance from temporal losses, and this pact is called the Old Testament. In another pact, God promised man spiritual blessings and deliverance from spiritual losses, and this is called the New Testament.

> I will make a new covenant, saith the Lord, with the house of Israel and with the house of Juda: not according to the covenant which I made with their fathers, in the day that I took them by the hand to bring them out of the land of Egypt.... But this shall be the covenant: ... I will give my law in their bosoms and I will write it in their hearts and I will be their God and they shall be my people (see Jer. 31:31–33).

Among the ancients, it was customary to pour out the blood of some victim in confirmation of a pact. This Moses did when, taking the blood, he sprinkled it upon the people and said, "This is the blood of the covenant which the Lord hath made with you" (Exod. 24:8). As the Old Testament or pact was thus confirmed in the figurative blood of oxen, so the New Testament or pact was confirmed in the blood of Christ, shed during His Passion.

2. *Testament* has another, more restricted meaning when it signifies the arrangement of an inheritance among the different heirs—a will. Testaments, in this sense, are confirmed only by the death of the testator. As St. Paul says, "For a testament is of force, after men are dead; otherwise it is as yet of no strength, whilst the testator liveth" (Heb. 9:17). God, in the beginning, made an arrangement of the eternal inheritance we were to receive, but under the figure of temporal goods. This is the Old Testament. But afterward He made the New Testament, explicitly promising the eternal inheritance, which indeed was confirmed by the blood of the death of Christ. And therefore, Our Lord, speaking of this, says, "This chalice is the new testament in my blood" (1 Cor. 11:25), as though to say, "By that which is contained in this chalice, the new testament, confirmed in the blood of Christ, is commemorated."

There are other things that make the blood of Christ precious:

- It is a cleansing of our sins and uncleanness. Jesus Christ "hath loved us and washed us from our sins in His own blood" (Apoc. 1:5).[13]
- It is our redemption: "Thou hast redeemed us … in Thy blood" (Apoc. 5:9).[14]
- It is the peacemaker between us and God and His angels, "making peace through the blood of His Cross, both as to the things that are on earth and the things that are in heaven" (Col. 1:20).

[13] RSV = Rev. 1:5.
[14] RSV = Rev. 5:9.

- It is a draught of life to all who receive it: "Drink ye all of this" (Matt. 26:27). That they "might drink the purest blood of the grape" (Deut. 32:14).
- It is the opening of the gate of Heaven: "Having therefore, brethren, a confidence in the entering into the holies by the blood of Christ" (Heb. 10:19)—that is to say, a continuous prayer for us to God. For His blood daily cries for us to the Father, as again we are told: "You are come to the sprinkling of blood which speaketh better than that of Abel" (Heb. 12:24). The blood of Abel called for punishment. The blood of Christ calls for pardon.
- It is deliverance of the saints from Hell: "Thou also by the blood of thy testament hast sent forth thy prisoners out of the pit, wherein is no water" (Zech. 9:11).

There was not any more
fitting way to free the
human race than through
the Passion of Christ

The suitability of any particular way for the attainment of a given end is reckoned according to the greater or lesser number of things useful to that end that the way in question brings about. The more things helpful to the end that the chosen method brings about, the better and more suitable is that method or way. Now, owing to the fact that it was through the Passion of Christ that man was delivered, many things, helpful to man's salvation, came together, in addition to his being freed from sin.

- Thanks to the fact that it was through the Passion that man was delivered, man learns how much God loves him and is thereby stimulated to that love of God, in which is to be found the perfection of man's salvation. "God commendeth His charity towards us: because when as yet we were sinners ... Christ died for us" (Rom. 5:8).
- In the Passion, He gave us an example of obedience, humility, constancy, justice, and other virtues also, all of which we must practice if we are to be saved. "Christ suffered for us, leaving you an example that you should follow His steps" (1 Pet. 2:21).
- Christ, by His Passion, not only delivered man from sin but also merited for man the grace that makes him acceptable to God and the glory of life with God for eternity.
- The fact that it is through the Passion that man has been saved brings home to man the need of keeping himself clear from sin.

Aquinas's Lenten Meditations

Man has only to realize that it was at the price of the blood of Christ that he was bought back from sin. "You are bought with a great price. Glorify and bear God in your body" (1 Cor. 6:20).

- The fact that the Passion was the way chosen heightens the dignity of human nature. As it was man who was deceived and conquered by the devil, so now it is man by whom the devil, in turn, is conquered. As it was man who once earned death, so it is man who, by dying, has overcome death. "Thanks be to God who hath given us the victory through Our Lord Jesus Christ" (1 Cor. 15:57).

Fifth Week of Lent

Passion Sunday

The Passion of Christ

*As Moses lifted up the serpent in the desert, so must the
Son of Man be lifted up: that whosoever believeth in
Him may not perish but may have life everlasting.*

—John 3:14–15

We may note here three things: (1) the figure of the Passion, (2) the mode of the Passion, and (3) the fruit of the Passion.

1. *The figure of the Passion: "As Moses lifted up the serpent in the desert"*
When the Jews said, "Our soul now loatheth this very light food" (Num. 21:5), the Lord sent serpents in punishment, and afterward, for a remedy, He commanded the brazen serpent to be made — as a remedy against the serpents and also as a figure of the Passion. It is the nature of a serpent to be poisonous, but the brazen serpent had no poison. It was but the figure of a poisonous serpent. So also Christ had no sin, which is the poison, but He had the likeness of sin. "God sent His own Son in the likeness of sinful flesh and of sin" (Rom. 8:3). Therefore, Christ had the effect of the serpent against the movements of our blazing desires.

2. *The mode of the Passion: "So must the Son of Man be lifted up"*
This refers to Christ's being raised upon the Cross. He willed to die lifted up:

- To purify the air: already He had purified the earth by the holiness of His living there; it still remained for Him to purify, by His dying there, the air.
- To triumph over the devils, who in the air, make their preparations to war on us
- To draw our hearts to His heart: "I, if I be lifted up from the earth will draw all things to myself (John 12:32). Since, in the

death of the Cross, He was exalted and since it was there that He overcame His enemies, we say that He was exalted rather than that He died. "He shall drink of the torrent by the way side; therefore He shall lift up the head" (Ps. 109:7).[15]

The Cross was the cause of His exaltation. "He became obedient unto death, even to the death of the cross, wherefore God hath exalted Him" (see Phil. 2:8).

3. The fruit of the Passion

The fruit is eternal life; whence Our Lord says Himself, "Whosoever believeth in Him, doing good works, may not perish, but may have life everlasting" (see John 3:16).

And this fruit corresponds to the fruit of the serpent that foreshadowed Him. For whoever looked upon the brazen serpent was delivered from the poison and his life was preserved. Now, the man who looks upon the Son of Man lifted up is the man who believes in Christ Crucified, and it is in this way that he is delivered from the poison that is sin and preserved for the life that is eternal.

[15] RSV = Ps. 110:7.

Passion Monday

The Passion of Christ is
a remedy against sin

We find in the Passion of Christ a remedy against all the evils that we incur through sin. Now these evils are five in number.

1. *We ourselves become unclean.* When a man commits any sin, he soils his soul, for just as virtue is the beauty of the soul, so sin is a stain upon it. "How happeneth it, O Israel, that thou art in thy enemies' land? Thou art grown old in a strange country, thou art defiled with the dead" (Bar. 3:10-11).

The Passion of Christ takes away this stain. For Christ, by His Passion, made of His blood a bath wherein He might wash sinners. The soul is washed with the blood of Christ in Baptism, for it is from the blood of Christ that the sacrament draws its power of giving new life. When, therefore, one who is baptized soils himself again by sin, he insults Christ and sins more deeply than before.

2. *We offend God.* As the man who is fleshly-minded loves what is beautiful to the flesh, so God loves spiritual beauty, the beauty of the soul. When the soul's beauty is defiled by sin, God is offended and holds the offender in hatred. But the Passion of Christ takes away this hatred, for it does what man himself could not possibly do—namely, it makes full satisfaction to God for the sin. The love and obedience of Christ was greater than the sin and rebellion of Adam.

3. *We ourselves are weakened.* Man believes that, once he has committed the sin, he will be able to keep from sin for the future. Experience

shows that what really happens is quite otherwise. The effect of the first sin is to weaken the sinner and make him still more inclined to sin. Sin dominates man more and more, and man, left to himself, whatever his powers, places himself in such a state that he cannot rise from it. Like a man who has thrown himself into a well, there he must lie, unless he is drawn up by some divine power. After the sin of Adam, then, our human nature was weaker, it had lost its perfection, and men were more prone to sinning.

But Christ, although He did not utterly make an end of this weakness, nevertheless greatly lessened it. Man is so strengthened by the Passion of Christ and the effect of Adam's sin is so weakened that he is no longer dominated by it. Helped by the grace of God, given him in the sacraments, which derive their power from the Passion of Christ, man is now able to make an effort and so rise up from his sins. Before the Passion of Christ, there were few who lived without mortal sin, but since the Passion, many have lived and do live without it.

4. *Liability to the punishment earned by sin.* This the justice of God demanded—namely, that for each sin, the sinner should be punished, the penalty to be measured according to the sin. Whence, since mortal sin is infinitely wicked, seeing that it is a sin against what is infinitely good—that is to say, God, whose commands the sin despises—the punishment due to mortal sin is infinite too.

But by His Passion, Christ took away from us this penalty, for He endured it Himself. "He Himself bore our sins [that is, the punishment due to us for our sins] in His body upon the tree" (1 Pet. 2:24).

So great was the power and value of the Passion of Christ that it was sufficient to expiate all the sins of all the world, reckoned by millions though they be. This is the reason Baptism frees the baptized from all their sins and why the priest can forgive sin. This is why the man who more and more fashions his life in conformity with the

Passion of Christ, and makes himself like to Christ in His Passion, attains an ever-fuller pardon and ever-greater graces.

5. *Banishment from the Kingdom.* Subjects who offend the king are sent into exile. So, too, man was expelled from Paradise. Adam, having sinned, was straightway thrown out and the gates barred against him. But, by His Passion, Christ opened those gates and called back the exiles from banishment. As the side of Christ opened to the soldier's lance, the gates of Heaven opened to man, and as Christ's blood flowed, the stain was washed out, God was appeased, our weakness was taken away, amends were made for our sins, and the exiles were recalled. Thus it was that Our Lord said immediately to the repentant thief, "This day thou shalt be with me in Paradise" (Luke 23:43). Such a thing was never before said to any man, not to Adam or to Abraham, or even to David. But *this day*, the day on which the gate is opened, the thief but asks and he finds, having confidence in the entering into the holies by the blood of Christ (Heb. 10:19).

Passion Tuesday

The burial of Christ

She hath wrought a good work upon me. She, in pouring
this ointment upon me, hath done it for my burial.

—Matt. 26:10, 12

It was right that Christ should be buried.

1. It proved that He had really died. No one is placed in the grave unless he is undeniably dead. And, as we read in St. Mark, Pilate, before he gave leave for Christ to be buried, made careful inquiry to assure himself that Christ was dead (15:44–45).

2. The very fact that Christ rose again from the grave gives a hope of rising again through Him to all others who lie in their graves. As it says in the Gospel, "All that are in the grave shall hear the voice of the Son of God. And they that hear shall live" (John 5:28, 25).

3. It was an example for those who, by the death of Christ, are spiritually dead to sin—for those, that is, who are hidden away from the turmoil of human affairs. So St. Paul says, "You are dead; and your life is hid with Christ in God" (Col. 3:3). So, too, those who are baptized—since, by the death of Christ, they die to sin—are, as it were, buried with Christ in their immersion, as St. Paul again says, "We are buried together with [Christ] by baptism into death" (Rom. 6:4).

As the death of Christ efficiently wrought our salvation, so, too, is His burial effective for us. St. Jerome, for example, says, "By the burial of Christ we all rise again," and explaining the words of Isaiah (53:9)—"He shall give the ungodly for His burial"—the Gloss says,

Aquinas's Lenten Meditations

"This means He shall give to God and the Father the nations lacking in filial devotion: for through His death and burial He has obtained possession of them."

The psalm says, "I am become as a man without help, free among the dead." (87:5–6).[16] Christ, by being buried, showed Himself free among the dead indeed, for His being enclosed in the tomb was not allowed to hinder His coming forth in the Resurrection.

---

[16] RSV = Ps. 88:4–5.

Passion Wednesday

On being buried spiritually

The sepulcher is a figure by which is signified the contemplation of heavenly things. So, St. Gregory, commenting on the words of Job (3:22)—"They rejoice exceedingly when they have found the grave"—says:

> As in the grave the body is hidden away when dead, so in divine contemplation there lies concealed the soul, dead to the world. There, at rest from the world's clamour, it lies, in a three days burial through, as it were, its triple immersion in baptism. Thou shalt hide them in the secret of thy face from the disturbance of men (Ps. 30:21). Those in great trouble, tormented with the hates of men, enter in spirit the presence of God and they are at rest.

Three things are required for this spiritual burial in God: (1) that the mind be perfected by the virtues, (2) that the mind be all bright and shining with purity, and (3) that it be wholly dead to this world. All these things are shown figuratively in the burial of Christ.

The first is shown in St. Mark's Gospel where we read how Mary Magdalen anointed Our Lord for His burial by anticipation, as it were. "She hath done what she could: she is come beforehand to anoint my body for the burial" (Mark 14:8). The ointment of precious spikenard (Mark 14:3) stands for the virtues, for it is a thing very precious, and in this life, nothing is more precious than the virtues. The soul that wishes to be holy and to be buried in divine contemplation, must

Aquinas's Lenten Meditations

first, then, anoint itself by the exercise of the virtues. Job says, "Thou shalt enter into the grave in abundance"—and the Gloss explains "the grave" as meaning here "divine contemplation"—"as a heap of wheat is brought in its season" (5:26), and the explanation given in the Gloss is that eternal contemplation is the prize of a life of action, and therefore it must be that the perfect, first of all, exercise their souls in the virtues and afterward bury them in the barn, where all quiet is gathered.

The second of the three things required is also noted in St. Mark, where we read that Joseph bought a winding sheet (15:46)—that is, a sheet of fine linen, which is brought to its dazzling whiteness only with great labor. Hence, it signifies that brightness of the soul, which also is not perfectly attained except with great labor. "He that is just, let him be justified still" (see Apoc. 22:11).[17] Let us "walk in newness of life" (Rom. 6:4), going from good to better, through the justice inaugurated by faith to the glory for which we hope. Therefore it is that men, bright with a spotless interior life, should be buried in the sepulcher of divine contemplation. St. Jerome, commenting on the words "Blessed are the clean of heart, for they shall see God" (Matt. 5:8), says, "The clean Lord is seen by the clean of heart."

The third point for consideration is given by St. John, where, in his Gospel, he writes, "Nicodemus also came, bringing a mixture of myrrh and aloes, about a hundred pound weight" (see 19:39). This hundred pounds' weight of myrrh and aloes, brought to preserve the dead body, symbolizes that perfect mortification of the external senses, the means by which the spirit, dead to the world, is preserved from the vices that would corrupt it. "Though our outward man is corrupted, yet the inward man is renewed day by day" (2 Cor. 4:16), which is as much as to say that the inward man is most thoroughly purified from vices by the fire of tribulation.

[17] RSV = Rev. 22:11.

Therefore, man's soul must first, with Christ, become dead to this world and afterward be buried with Him in the hiding place of divine contemplation. St. Paul says, "You are dead" with Christ, to the things that are vain and fleeting, "and your life is hid with Christ in God" (Col. 3:3).

Passion Thursday

Which is the greatest sign of His love our Lord has given us?

It would seem that Christ gave us a greater sign of His love by giving us His body as our food than by suffering for us. For the love that will be in the life to come is a more perfect thing than the love that is in this life. And the benefit that Christ bestows on us by giving us His body as food is more like to the love of the life to come, in which we shall fully enjoy God. The Passion that Christ underwent for us is, on the other hand, more like to the love that is of this life, in which we, too, are to suffer for Christ. Therefore, it is a greater sign of Christ's love for us that He delivered His body to us as our food than that He suffered for us.

Nevertheless, it is an argument against this that in St. John's Gospel, Our Lord Himself says, "Greater love than this no man hath, that a man lay down His life for his friends" (John 15:13).

The strongest of human loves is the love with which a man loves himself. Therefore, this love must be the measure, by comparison with which we estimate the love by which a man loves others than himself. Now, the extent of a man's love for another is shown by the extent of good desired for himself that he forgoes for his friend. As Holy Scripture says, "He that neglecteth a loss for the sake of a friend is just" (Prov. 12:26). Now a man wishes well to himself as to three things: his soul, his body, and things outside himself.

It is then already a sign of love that, for another, a man is willing to suffer loss of things outside himself. It is a greater sign if he is also willing to suffer loss in his body for another, that is, by bearing the burden of work or undergoing punishment. It is the greatest of all signs of love if a man is willing, by dying for his friend, to lay down his very life.

Therefore, that Christ, in suffering for us, laid down His life was the greatest of all signs that He loved us. That He has given us His body for our food in the sacrament does not entail for Him any loss. It follows, then, that the first is the greater sign. Also, this sacrament is a kind of memorial and figure of the Passion of Christ. But the truth is always greater than that which figures it; the thing is always greater than the memorial that recalls it.

The showing forth of the body of Christ in the sacrament has about it, it is true, a certain figure of the love with which God loves us in the life to come. But Christ's Passion is associated with that love itself, by which God calls us from perdition to the life to come. The love of God, however, is not greater in the life to come than it is in this present life.

Passion Friday

Our Lady's suffering
in the Passion

Thy own soul a sword shall pierce.

—Luke 2:35

In these words, there is noted for us the close association of Our Lady with the Passion of Christ. Four things especially made the Passion most bitter for her.

- Firstly, the goodness of her Son, "who did no sin" (1 Pet. 2:22).
- Secondly, the cruelty of those who crucified Him—shown, for example, in this: that as He lay dying, they refused Him even water, nor would they allow His Mother, who would most lovingly have given it, to help Him.
- Thirdly, the disgrace of the punishment: "Let us condemn him to a most shameful death" (Wisd. 2:20).
- Fourthly, the cruelty of the torment: "O ye that pass by the way, attend and see if there be any sorrow like to my sorrow" (Lam. 1:12).

The words of Simeon, "Thy own soul a sword shall pierce," Origen, and other Doctors with him, explain with reference to the pain felt by Our Lady in the Passion of Christ. St. Ambrose, however, says that by "the sword" is signified Our Lady's prudence, thanks to which she was not without knowledge of the heavenly mystery. For the word of God is a living thing, strong and keener than the keenest sword (see Heb. 4:12).

Other writers again—St. Augustine, for example—understand by "the sword" the stupefaction that overcame Our Lady at the death of her Son: not the doubt that goes with lack of faith but a certain fluctuation of bewilderment, a staggering of the mind. St. Basil, too, says that as Our Lady stood by the Cross with all the detail of the Passion before her, and in her mind the testimony of Gabriel, the message that words cannot tell of her divine conception, and all the vast array of miracles, her mind swayed, for she saw Him the victim of such vileness and yet knew Him for the author of such wonders.

Although Our Lady knew by faith that it was God's will that Christ should suffer, and although she brought her will into unity with God's will in this matter, as the saints do, nevertheless, sadness filled her soul at the death of Christ. This was because her lower will revolted at the particular thing she had willed, and this is not contrary to perfection.

Passion Saturday

How each of us should
wash one another's feet

*If I then, being your Lord and Master, have washed
your feet, you also ought to wash one another's feet."*

—John 13:14

Our Lord wishes that His disciples shall imitate His example. He says, therefore, "If I, who am the greater, being your Master and the Lord, have washed your feet, you also, all the more who are the less, who are disciples, slaves even, ought to wash one another's feet." "Whosoever will be the greater among you, let him be your minister.... Even as the Son of Man is not come to be ministered unto, but to minister" (Matt. 20:26, 28).

St. Augustine says every man ought to wash the feet of his fellows, either actually or in spirit. And it is by far the best, and true beyond all controversy, that we should do it actually, lest Christians scorn to do what Christ did. For when a man bends his body to the feet of a brother, human feeling is stirred up in his very heart, or, if it be there already, it is strengthened. If we cannot actually wash his feet, at least we can do it in spirit. The washing of the feet signifies the washing away of stains. You therefore wash the feet of your brother when, as far as lies in your power, you wash away his stains. And this you may do in three ways:

1. By forgiving the offenses he has done to you: "Forgiving one another, if any have a complaint against another: even as the Lord hath forgiven you, so do you also" (Col. 3:13).

2. By praying for the forgiveness of his sin, as St. James bids us: "Pray for one another that you may be saved" (see 5:16). This way of washing, like the first, is open to all the faithful.

3. The third way is for prelates, who should wash by forgiving
sins through the authority of the keys, according to the
Gospel: "Receive ye the Holy Ghost; whose sins you shall
forgive, they are forgiven them" (John 20:22-23).

We can also say that in this one act, Our Lord showed all the
works of mercy. He who gives bread to the hungry, washes his feet,
as also does the man who harbors the harborless or he who clothes
the naked—"communicating to the necessities of the saints" (Rom.
12:13).

Holy Week

Holy Week: Palm Sunday

Christ's Passion serves
us as an example

The Passion of Christ is, by itself, sufficient to form us in every virtue. For whoever wishes to live perfectly need do no more than scorn what Christ scorned on the Cross and to desire what He there desired. There is no virtue of which, from the Cross, Christ does not give us an example.

If you seek an example of charity, "Greater love than this no man hath, than that a man lay down his life for his friends" (John 15:13), and this Christ did on the Cross. And since it was for us that He gave His life, it should not be burdensome to bear for Him whatever evils come our way. "What shall I render to the Lord, for all the things that He hath rendered to me?" (Ps. 115:12).[18]

If you seek an example of patience, in the Cross you find the best of all. Great patience shows itself in two ways: either when a man suffers great evils patiently or when he suffers what he could avoid and forbears to avoid. Now, Christ on the Cross suffered great evils. "O all ye that pass by the way, attend and see, if there be any sorrow like to my sorrow" (Lam. 1:12). And He suffered them patiently, for "when He suffered, He threatened not" (1 Pet. 2:23) but "led as a sheep to the slaughter," He was "dumb as a lamb before His shearer" (Isa. 53:7).

Also it was in His power to avoid the suffering, and He did not avoid it. "Thinkest thou that I cannot ask my Father, and He will give

[18] RSV = Ps. 116:12.

me presently more than twelve legions of angels?" (Matt. 26:53). The patience of Christ on the Cross, then, was the greatest patience ever shown. "Let us run by patience to the fight proposed to us: looking on Jesus, the author and finisher of faith, who having joy set before Him, endured the cross, despising the shame" (Heb. 12:1-2).

If you seek an example of humility, look at the Crucified. For it is God who wills to be judged and to die at the will of Pontius Pilate. "Thy cause hath been judged as that of the wicked" (Job 36:17). Truly as that of the wicked, for "Let us condemn him to a most shameful death" (Wisd. 2:20). The Lord willed to die for the slave, the life of the angels for man.

If you seek an example of obedience, follow Him who became "obedient unto death" (Phil. 2:8), "for as by the disobedience of one man, many were made sinners; so also by the obedience of one, many shall be made just" (Rom. 5:19).

If you seek an example in the scorning of the things of this world, follow Him who is the King of Kings and the Lord of Lords, in whom are all the treasures of wisdom. Lo! on the Cross He hangs naked, humiliated, spit upon, beaten, crowned with thorns, sated with gall and vinegar, and dead. "My garments they parted among them; and upon my vesture they cast lots" (Ps. 21:19).[19]

It was error to crave for honors, for He was exposed to blows and to mockery. Error to seek titles and decorations, for "platting a crown of thorns, they put it upon His head, and a reed in His right hand. And bowing the knee before Him, they mocked Him, saying, 'Hail, king of the Jews'" (Matt. 27:29). Error to cling to pleasures and comfort for "they gave me gall for my food, and in my thirst they gave me vinegar to drink" (Ps. 68:22).[20]

[19] RSV = Ps. 22:18.
[20] RSV = Ps. 69:21.

Monday in Holy Week

It is necessary that we be wholly clean

1. "If I wash thee not, thou shalt have no part with me" (John 13:8). No one can be made a sharer in the inheritance of eternity, a co-heir with Christ, unless he is spiritually cleansed, for in the Apocalypse it is so stated: "There shall not enter into it anything defiled" (21:27),[21] and in the Psalms we read, "Lord, who shall dwell in Thy tabernacle?" (14:1).[22] "Who shall ascend into the mountain of the Lord; or who shall stand in His holy place? The innocent in hands, and clean of heart" (23:3-4).[23]

It is, therefore, as though Our Lord said, "If I wash thee not, thou shalt not be cleansed, and if thou art not cleansed, thou shalt have no part with me."

2. Simon Peter saith to Him: "Lord, not only my feet but also my hands and my head" (John 13:9). Peter, utterly stricken, offers his whole self to be washed, so confounded is he with love and with fear. We read, in fact, in the book called *The Journeying of Clement*, that Peter used to be so overcome by the bodily presence of Our Lord, which he had most fervently loved, that whenever, after Our Lord's Ascension, the memory of that dearest presence and most holy company came to him, he used so to melt into tears that his cheeks seemed all worn out with them.

[21] RSV = Rev. 21:27.
[22] RSV = Ps. 15:1.
[23] RSV = Ps. 24:3-4.

Aquinas's Lenten Meditations

We can consider three parts in man's body: the head, which is the highest; the feet, which are the lowest part; and the hands, which lie in between. In the interior man—that is to say, in the soul—there are likewise three parts. Corresponding to the head, there is the higher reason, the power by means of which the soul clings to God. For the hands, there is the lower reason, by which the soul operates in good works. For the feet, there are the senses and the feelings and desires arising from them. Now, Our Lord knew the disciples to be clean as far as the head was concerned, for He knew they were joined to God by faith and by charity. He knew their hands also were clean, for He knew their good works. But as to their feet, He knew that the disciples were still somewhat entangled in those inclinations to earthly things that derive out of the life of the senses.

Peter, alarmed by Our Lord's warning ("If I wash thee not, thou shalt have no part with me"), not only consented that his feet should be washed but begged that his hands and his head should be washed too.

"Lord," he said, "not only my feet, but also my hands and my head," as though to say, "I know not whether hands and head need to be washed. 'For I am not conscious to myself of anything, yet am I not hereby justified' [1 Cor. 4:4]. Therefore, I am ready not only for my feet (that is, those inclinations that arise out of the life of my senses) to be washed but also my hands (that is, my works) and my head (that is, my higher reason)."

3. "Jesus saith to him: He that is washed needeth not but to wash his feet, but is clean wholly. And you are clean" (John 13:10). Origen, commenting on this text, says that the Apostles were clean but needed to be yet cleaner. For reason should ever desire gifts that are better still, should ever set itself to achieve the very heights of virtue, should aspire to shine with the brightness of justice itself. "He that is holy, let him be sanctified still" (Apoc. 22:11).[24]

[24] RSV = Rev. 22:11.

Tuesday in Holy Week

Christ preparing to wash the Apostles' feet

He riseth from supper, and layeth aside His garments,
and having taken a towel, girded Himself.

—John 13:4

1. Christ, in His lowly office, shows Himself truly to be a servant, in keeping with His own words: "The Son of Man is not come to be ministered unto, but to minister, and to give His life a redemption for many" (Matt. 20:28).

Three things are looked for in a good servant or minister:

1. He should be careful to keep before him the numerous details in which his serving may so easily fall short. Now, for a servant to sit or to lie down during his service is to make this necessary supervision impossible. Hence it is that servants stand. And therefore, the Gospel says of Our Lord, "He riseth from supper." Our Lord Himself also asks us, "For which is greater, he that sitteth at table or he that serveth?" (Luke 22:27).

2. He should show dexterity in doing at the right time all the things his particular office calls for. Now, elaborate dress is a hindrance to this. Therefore, Our Lord "layeth aside His garments." And this was foreshadowed in the Old Testament when Abraham chose servants who were well appointed (Gen. 14:14).

3. He should be prompt, having ready to hand all the things he needs. St. Luke says of Martha that she was busy about much serving (10:40). This is why Our Lord, having taken a towel, girded Himself. Thus, He was ready not only to wash the feet but also to dry them. So He ("who came from God and goeth to God" [John 13:3]), as He washes their feet, crushes down forever our swollen human self-importance.

2. "After that, He putteth water into a basin, and began to wash" (John 13:5). We are given for our consideration this service of Christ; and in three ways His humility is set for our example.

1. The kind of service this was, for it was the lowest kind of service of all: the Lord of all majesty bending to wash the feet of His slaves.

2. The number of services it contained, for, we are told, He put water into a basin, He washed their feet, He dried them, and so forth.

3. The method of doing the service, for He did not do it through others, nor even with others helping Him; He did the service Himself. "The greater thou art, the more humble thyself in all things" (Ecclus. 3:20).[25]

---

[25] RSV = Sir. 3:18.

Wednesday in Holy Week

Three things are symbolized by the washing of the feet

He putteth "water into a basin, and began to wash the feet of the disciples, and to wipe them with the towel wherewith he was girded" (John 13:5). There are three things which this can be taken to symbolize:

1. The pouring of the water into the basin is a symbol of the pouring out of His blood upon the earth. Since the blood of Jesus has a power of cleansing, it may, in a sense, be called water. The reason why water, as well as blood, came out of His side, was to show that this blood could wash away sin.

Again we might take the water as a figure of Christ's Passion. "He putteth water into a basin": that is, by faith and devotion, He stamped into the minds of faithful followers the memory of His Passion. "Remember my poverty, and transgression, the wormwood and the gall" (Lam. 3:19).

2. By the words "and began to wash," it is human imperfection that is symbolized. For the Apostles, after living with Christ, were certainly more perfect, and yet they needed to be washed; there were still stains upon them. We are here made to understand that whatever the degree of any man's perfection, he still needs to be made more perfect still; He is still contracting uncleanness of some kind to some extent. So in the book of Proverbs, we read, "Who can say, 'My heart is clean I am pure from sin'?" (Prov. 20:9).

Nevertheless, the Apostles and the just have this kind of uncleanness only in their feet.

Aquinas's Lenten Meditations

There are, however, others who are infected, not only in their feet, but wholly and entirely. Those who make their bed upon the soiling attractions of the world are made wholly unclean thereby. Those who wholly—that is to say, with their senses and with their wills—cleave to their desire of earthly things: these are wholly unclean.

But they who do not thus lie down—they who stand, that is; they who, in mind and in desire, are tending toward heavenly things—contract this uncleanness in their feet. Whoever stands must, necessarily, touch the earth, at least with his feet. And we, too, in this life, where we must, to maintain life, make use of earthly things, cannot but contract a certain uncleanness, at least as far as those desires and inclinations that begin in our senses are concerned.

Therefore, Our Lord commanded His disciples to shake off the dust from their feet (Matt. 10:14). The text says, "He began to wash," because this washing away on earth of the affection for earthly things is only a beginning. It is only in the life to come that it will be really complete.

Thus, by putting water into the basin, the pouring out of His blood is signified, and by His beginning to wash the feet of His disciples is signified the washing away of our sins.

3. There is symbolized finally Our Lord's taking upon Him the punishment due to our sins. Not only did He wash away our sins, but He also took upon Himself the punishment that they had earned; for our pains and our penances would not suffice were they not founded in the merit and the power of the Passion of Christ. And this is shown in His wiping the feet of the disciples with the linen towel—that is, the towel that is His body.

Maundy Thursday

The Last Supper

It was most fitting that the sacrament of the body of the Lord should have been instituted at the Last Supper:

1. Because of what that sacrament contains: for that which is contained in it is Christ Himself. When Christ, in His natural appearance, was about to depart from His disciples, He left Himself to them in a sacramental appearance, just as, in the absence of the emperor, there is exhibited the emperor's image. Whence St. Eusebius says:

> Since the body He had assumed was about to be taken away from their bodily sight, and was about to be carried to the stars, it was necessary that, on the day of His last supper, He should consecrate for us the sacrament of His body and blood, so that what, as a price, was offered once should, through a mystery, be worshipped unceasingly.

2. Because without faith in the Passion, there can never be salvation. Therefore, it is necessary that there should be, forever, among men something that would represent the Lord's Passion, and the chief of such representative things in the Old Testament was the Paschal lamb. To this there succeeded in the New Testament the sacrament of the Eucharist, which is commemorative of the past Passion of the Lord as the Paschal lamb was a foreshadowing of the Passion to come.

And therefore was it most fitting that, on the very eve of the Passion, the old sacrament of the Paschal lamb having been celebrated, Our Lord should institute the new sacrament.

Aquinas's Lenten Meditations

3. Because the last words of departing friends remain longest in the memory, our love being at such moments most tenderly alert. Nothing can be greater in the realm of sacrifice than that of the Body and Blood of Christ, no offering can be more effective. And hence, in order that the sacrament might be held in all the more veneration, it was in His last leave-taking of the Apostles that Our Lord instituted it.

Hence, St. Augustine says, "Our Savior, to bring before our minds with all His power the heights and the depths of this sacrament, willed, ere He left the disciples to go forth to His Passion, to fix it in their hearts and their memories as His last act."

Let us note that this sacrament has a threefold meaning:

1. In regard to the past, it is commemorative of the Lord's Passion, which was a true sacrifice, and because of this, the sacrament is called a sacrifice.

2. In regard to a fact of our own time—that is, to the unity of the Church and that through this sacrament mankind should be gathered together. Because of this, the sacrament is called Communion.

    St. John Damascene says the sacrament is called Communion because by means of it, we communicate with Christ—and this because we hereby share in His Body and in His divinity—and because by it we are communicated to and united with one another.

3. In regard to the future, the sacrament foreshadows that enjoyment of God that shall be ours in our fatherland. On this account, the sacrament is called Viaticum, since it provides us with the means of journeying to that fatherland.

Good Friday

The death of Christ: that Christ should die was expedient

It was expedient that Christ should die:

1. To make our redemption complete, for, although any suffering of Christ had an infinite value, because of its union with His divinity, it was not by no matter which of His sufferings that the redemption of mankind was made complete but only by His death. So the Holy Spirit declared speaking through the mouth of Caiaphas: "It is expedient for you that one man shall die for the people" (John 11:50). Whence St. Augustine says, "Let us stand in wonder, rejoice, be glad, love, praise, and adore since it is by the death of our Redeemer that we have been called from death to life, from exile to our own land, from mourning to joy."

2. To increase our faith, our hope, and our charity: With regard to faith, the psalm says, "I am alone until I pass" from this world, that is, to the Father (140:10).[26] "When I shall have passed to the Father, then shall I be multiplied. 'Unless the grain of wheat falling into the ground die, itself remaineth alone'" (John 12:24–25).

As to the increase of hope St. Paul writes, "He that spared not even His own Son, but delivered Him up for us all, how hath He not also, with Him, given us all things?" (Rom. 8:32). God cannot deny us this, for to give us all things is less than to give His own Son to death for us. St. Bernard says, "Who is not carried away to hope and confidence in prayer, when he looks on the crucifix and

[26] RSV = Ps. 141:10.

sees how Our Lord hangs there, the head bent as though to kiss, the arms outstretched in an embrace, the hands pierced to give, the side opened to love, the feet nailed to remain with us."

"Come, my dove, in the clefts of the rock" (see Cant. 2:14).[27] It is in the wounds of Christ that the Church builds her nest and waits, for it is in the Passion of Our Lord that she places her hope of salvation and thereby trusts to be protected from the craft of the falcon—that is, of the devil.

With regard to the increase of charity, Holy Scripture says, "At noon he burneth the earth" (Ecclus. 43:3),[28] that is to say, in the fervor of His Passion, He burns up all mankind with His love. So St. Bernard says, "The chalice thou didst drink, O good Jesus, maketh Thee lovable above all things." The work of our redemption, easily brushing aside all hindrances, calls out in return the whole of our love. This it is that more gently draws out our devotion, builds it up more straightly, guards it more closely, and fires it with greater ardor.

[27] RSV = Song of Sol. 2:14.
[28] RSV = Sir. 43:3.

Holy Saturday

Why our Lord went
down to Limbo

From the descent of Christ to Hell we may learn, for our instruction, four things:

1. Firm hope in God: No matter what the trouble in which a man finds himself, he should always put trust in God's help and rely on it. There is no trouble greater than to find oneself in Hell. If, then, Christ freed those who were in Hell, any man who is a friend of God cannot but have great confidence that he, too, shall be freed from whatever anxiety holds him. Wisdom "forsook not the just when he was sold but delivered him from sinners; she went down with him into the pit and in bands she left him not" (Wisd. 10:13-14). And since to His servants God gives a special assistance, he who serves God should have still greater confidence. He that feareth the Lord shall tremble at nothing and shall not be afraid: for He is his hope (Ecclus. 34:16).[29]

2. We ought to conceive fear and to rid ourselves of presumption, for although Christ suffered for sinners and went down into Hell to set them free, He did not set all sinners free but only those who were free of mortal sin. Those who had died in mortal sin He left there. Wherefore for those who have gone down to Hell in mortal sin, there remains no hope of pardon. They shall be in Hell as the holy Fathers are in Heaven—that is, forever.

3. We ought to be full of care. Christ went down into Hell for our salvation, and we should be careful frequently to go down there too,

[29] RSV = Sir. 43:14.

turning over in our minds Hell's pain and penalties, as did the holy king Hezekiah, as we read in the prophecy of Isaiah: "I said: 'In the midst of my days I shall go to the gates of hell' " (38:10).

Those who, in their meditation, often go down to Hell during life will not easily go down there at death. Such meditations are a powerful arm against sin and a useful aid to bring a man back from sin. Daily we see men kept from evildoing by the fear of the law's punishments. How much greater care should they not take on account of the punishment of Hell, greater in its duration, in its bitterness, and in its variety. "Remember thy last end and thou shalt never sin" (Ecclus. 7:40).[30]

4. The fact is, for us, an example of love. Christ went down into Hell to set free those who were His own. We, too, therefore, should go down there to help our own. For those who are in Purgatory are themselves unable to do anything, and therefore we ought to help them. Truly he would be a harsh man indeed who failed to come to the aid of a kinsman who lay in prison here on earth. How much harsher, then, the man who will not aid the friend who is in Purgatory, for there is no comparison between the pains there and the pains of this world. "Have pity on me, have pity on me, at least you my friends, because the hand of the Lord hath touched me" (Job 19:21).

We help the souls in Purgatory chiefly by these three means: by Masses, by prayers, and by almsgiving. Nor is it wonderful that we can do so, for even in this world, a friend can make satisfaction for a friend.

[30] RSV = Sir. 7:36.

About the Author

St. Thomas Aquinas was born in Naples around 1225. He studied at Monte Cassino Abbey and the University of Naples. In 1244, against the wishes of his family, he entered the Dominican Order. The Dominicans sent Thomas to the University of Paris to study with the Aristotelian scholar Albert the Great. In 1252, Thomas began his teaching career. Through many formal academic disputations, through his preaching, and in more than a hundred written volumes, St. Thomas gave his reason unreservedly to the service of Christian revelation. Relying heavily on the Greek philosopher Aristotle, Thomas showed that Christian faith is credible, defensible, and intelligible.

Moreover, St. Thomas's prodigious scholarship nurtured his own spiritual development. He prayed intensely and was known to suffer the terrible spiritual trials and sublime consolations of the true ascetic and contemplative.

St. Thomas died on March 7, 1274, at the age of fifty. He was canonized in 1323 and proclaimed a Doctor of the Universal Church in 1567. In his encyclical *Æterni Patris* (August 4, 1879), Pope Leo XIII called on all men to "restore the golden wisdom of St. Thomas and to spread it far and wide for the defense and beauty of the Catholic Faith, for the good of society, and for the advantage of all sciences."

Sophia Institute

Sophia Institute is a nonprofit institution that seeks to nurture the spiritual, moral, and cultural life of souls and to spread the gospel of Christ in conformity with the authentic teachings of the Roman Catholic Church.

Sophia Institute Press fulfills this mission by offering translations, reprints, and new publications that afford readers a rich source of the enduring wisdom of mankind.

Sophia Institute also operates the popular online resource CatholicExchange.com. *Catholic Exchange* provides world news from a Catholic perspective as well as daily devotionals and articles that will help readers to grow in holiness and live a life consistent with the teachings of the Church.

In 2013, Sophia Institute launched Sophia Institute for Teachers to renew and rebuild Catholic culture through service to Catholic education. With the goal of nurturing the spiritual, moral, and cultural life of souls, and an abiding respect for the role and work of teachers, we strive to provide materials and programs that are at once enlightening to the mind and ennobling to the heart; faithful and complete, as well as useful and practical.

Sophia Institute gratefully recognizes the Solidarity Association for preserving and encouraging the growth of our apostolate over the course of many years. Without their generous and timely support, this book would not be in your hands.

www.SophiaInstitute.com
www.CatholicExchange.com
www.SophiaInstituteforTeachers.org

Sophia Institute Press is a registered trademark of Sophia Institute.
Sophia Institute is a tax-exempt institution as defined by the
Internal Revenue Code, Section 501(c)(3). Tax ID 22-2548708.